MENTAL HEALTH AND ANCIENT EGYPTIAN PSYCHOLOGY GUIDEBOOK

THE AMENEMOPET WISDOM TEXT TRANSFORMATION MANUAL

A Self-Paced Practical Integration Workbook

Companion to:

Mental Health and Ancient Egyptian Psychology:
New Translation of Sage Amenemopet's Wisdom Text
of Optimal Physical and Spiritual Transformation
For Self-Mastery & Enlightenment

About the Author - Dr. Muata Ashby

Dr. Muata Ashby is a distinguished spiritual teacher, scholar, philosopher, and author whose groundbreaking work has significantly contributed to the understanding of Ancient Egyptian (Kemetic) spirituality and its profound connections to world religions. With over 70 books published on yoga philosophy, religious philosophy, and social philosophy based on ancient African principles, Dr. Ashby has established himself as the leading authority in comparative religious studies with a specialized focus on Ancient Egyptian wisdom traditions.

Academic Credentials and Foundation

Dr. Ashby holds a Doctor of Philosophy Degree in Religion and a Doctor of Divinity Degree from the American Institute of Holistic Theology, as well as a Master's degree in Liberal Arts and Religious Studies from Thomas Edison State College. His extensive academic background is complemented by comprehensive independent research spanning Egyptian Yoga, Indian Yoga, Chinese Yoga, Buddhism, mystical psychology, and Christian Mysticism. He has also engaged in Post Graduate research in advanced Jnana, Bhakti, and Kundalini Yogas at the Yoga Research Foundation.

Institutional Leadership and Innovation

As the founder of the Sema Institute, a non-profit organization dedicated to spreading the wisdom of Ancient Egyptian mystical traditions, and the Kemetic University along with the Egyptian Mystery School, Dr. Ashby has developed innovative approaches to teaching ancient wisdom using traditional temple teaching methods alongside modern technologies. Dr Ashby has taught at Florida International University in the capacity of Adjunct professor. Currently he teaches through the online school he created called *"Kemet University"*. When functioning in academic settings, he is addressed as Dr. Muata Ashby.

Scholarly Contributions and Research

Dr. Ashby began his groundbreaking research in the 1990s, investigating correlations between Ancient Egyptian and Indian spiritual traditions, which became the catalyst for his successful "Egyptian Yoga" book series launched in 1994. A leading advocate of the concept that advanced social and religious philosophies existed in ancient Africa comparable to Eastern traditions such as Vedanta, Buddhism, Confucianism, and Taoism, he has lectured and written extensively on these correlations, promoting greater cross-cultural understanding and spiritual advancement. His scholarly work encompasses extensive research into Ancient Egyptian philosophy and social order, with particular expertise in Maat philosophy—the ethical foundation of Ancient Egyptian society. Dr. Ashby has studied anthropology and Ancient Egyptian language, spending thousands of hours investigating and translating texts with a special interest in discovering the Ancient Egyptian Religious Philosophy (*sebait*) that fueled the development of Ancient Egyptian society and spirituality.

Revolutionary Translation Method

I have developed a unique and revolutionary form of translating ancient texts called "Trilinear Translation," which goes beyond the basic Egyptological interlinear format to expose greater depth of insight through deeper contextual exposition. This innovative method provides three levels of translation: phonetic transliteration, direct word-for-word translation, and contextual translation that incorporates philosophical, mythological, and historical background insights, making ancient wisdom more accessible to contemporary readers.

Musical and Artistic Contributions

Since 1999, Dr. Ashby has researched Ancient Egyptian musical theory and created a series of musical compositions that explore this unique area of music from ancient Africa and its connection to world music. As an accomplished lecturer, musician, artist, poet, painter, screenwriter, and playwright, he brings a multidisciplinary approach to his scholarly work, enriching the understanding of ancient wisdom through various artistic expressions.

Global Impact and Outreach

Dr. Ashby has lectured extensively throughout the United States, Europe, and Africa, sharing his insights on ancient wisdom traditions with diverse audiences. His work has reached practitioners and scholars worldwide, establishing him as an internationally recognized authority on Ancient Egyptian spirituality and its practical applications for contemporary spiritual seekers.

Collaborative Partnership

Dr. Ashby works closely with his spiritual and life partner, Dr. Dja Ashby (formerly Karen Clarke), who serves as co-founder of the Sema Institute and director of C.M. Book Publishing. Together, they have been married for over 40 years and continue to advance the dissemination of Ancient Egyptian wisdom through their collaborative efforts in publishing, teaching, and spiritual guidance.

Current Work and Legacy

In his recent work, Dr. Ashby has focused intensively on the temples of Aset (Isis) and Asar (Osiris), producing detailed photographic documentation and original translations of hieroglyphic scriptures. His commitment to making ancient wisdom accessible to modern practitioners is evident in his development of comprehensive study programs that bridge the gap between ancient temple teachings and contemporary spiritual practice.

The present monumental work on the Scripture of Ra and Hetheru, from the Tomb of Sety 1st, represents Dr. Ashby's continued dedication to translating and interpreting Ancient Egyptian spiritual texts with a focus on their mystical and practical applications for contemporary spiritual seekers. Through his extensive scholarship, innovative translation methods, and deep spiritual understanding, Dr. Ashby continues to illuminate the profound wisdom of Ancient Egypt for a new generation of practitioners and scholars seeking authentic spiritual transformation.

Dr. Ashby's life work demonstrates that the wisdom of ancient Africa—particularly Ancient Egypt—offers profound insights into the nature of consciousness, spiritual development, and the path to enlightenment that remain as relevant today as they were thousands of years ago.

MORE BOOKS BY THE AUTHOR:

amazon.com/author/muataashby

Sema Institute

P.O. Box 570459

Miami, Florida, 33257

(305) 378-6253 Fax: (305) 378-6253

First U.S. edition ⓒ 2025 By Reginald Muata Ashby

All rights reserved. No part of this book may be used or reproduced in any manner whatsoever without written permission (address above) except in the case of brief quotations embodied in critical articles and reviews. All inquiries may be addressed to the address above.

The author is available for group lectures and individual counseling. For further information contact the publisher.

Ashby, Muata (2025)

MENTAL HEALTH AND ANCIENT EGYPTIAN PSYCHOLOGY GUIDEBOOK: The Amenemopet Wisdom Text Transformation Manual, a Self-paced Practical Integration Workbook ISBN: **9781937016814**

Library of Congress Cataloging in Publication Data

Ancient Egyptian Psychology Wisdom of Amenemopet Guidebook

TABLE OF CONTENTS

About the Author - Dr. Muata Ashby 3
HOW TO USE THIS WORKBOOK 12
    The Module System 12
    The Practice Progression 12
    Key Terms You'll Encounter 12
MODULE 1: The Foundation of Wisdom Philosophy for Life Transformation 16
    Quick Chapter Overview 16
    Daily Reflection Practice 17
    Daily Contemplation Practice 18
    Aryu Pattern Recognition Exercise 20
    Deep Reflection Questions 22
    Visual Summary: The Three Levels of Mind 24
    Module Completion Reflection 25
MODULE 2: The Psychology of Wisdom Absorption and Aryu Purification 26
    Quick Chapter Overview 26
    Daily Reflection Practice 27
    Daily Contemplation Practice 28
    Aryu Pattern Recognition Exercise 30
    Deep Reflection Questions 32
    Visual Summary: The Three Levels of Mind 34
    Module Completion Reflection 35
MODULE 3: The Cosmic Psychology of Unrighteous Action and the Enemy of Life 36
    Quick Chapter Overview 36
    Daily Reflection Practice 37
    Daily Contemplation Practice 38
    Aryu Pattern Recognition Exercise 40
    Deep Reflection Questions 41
    Visual Summary: The Three Levels of Mind 43
    Module Completion Reflection 44

MODULE 4: The Sacred Navigation of Life's Journey - Conscious Effort 45
- Quick Chapter Overview 45
- Daily Reflection Practice 46
- Daily Contemplation Practice 47
- Aryu Pattern Recognition Exercise 49
- Deep Reflection Questions 50
- Module Completion Reflection 52

MODULE 5: The Sacred Art of Spiritual Discernment - Conscious Disassociation 53
- Quick Chapter Overview 53
- Daily Reflection Practice 54
- Daily Contemplation Practice 55
- Aryu Pattern Recognition Exercise 57
- Deep Reflection Questions 58
- Visual Summary: The Three Levels of Mind 60
- Module Completion Reflection 61

MODULE 6: The Psychology of Spiritual Receptivity and Silent Mind and Feelings 62
- Quick Chapter Overview 62
- Daily Reflection Practice 63
- Daily Contemplation Practice 64
- Aryu Pattern Recognition Exercise 66
- Deep Reflection Questions 67
- Visual Summary: The Three Levels of Mind 69
- Module Completion Reflection 70

MODULE 7: The Psychology of Inner Fulfillment Through Divine Communion 71
- Quick Chapter Overview 71
- Daily Reflection Practice 72
- Daily Contemplation Practice 73
- Aryu Pattern Recognition Exercise 75
- Deep Reflection Questions 76
- Visual Summary: The Three Levels of Mind 78
- Module Completion Reflection 79

MODULE 8: Maintaining Awareness of All-Encompassing Divinity - Deliberate Neberdjer Recognition 80

Quick Chapter Overview 80
Daily Reflection Practice 81
Daily Contemplation Practice 82
Aryu Pattern Recognition Exercise... 84
Deep Reflection Questions 85
Visual Summary: The Three Levels of Mind 87
Module Completion Reflection 88

MODULE 9: THE PRACTICE OF SAU-NEBERDJER CONSCIOUSNESS MEDITATION 89
Understanding This Transition 89
Quick Chapter Overview 89
Daily Meditation Practice 90
TWO EXERCISES TO BEGIN THE PRACTICE OF INTROSPECTION 90
COMPLETE PRACTICE INSTRUCTIONS (20-30 minutes) 92
Working With Challenges 93
Practice Log 94
Visual Summary: The Three Levels of Mind 95
Module Completion Reflection 96

MODULE 10: Divine Providence Versus Worldly Scheming 97
Daily Reflection Practice 97
Daily Contemplation Practice (15-20 minutes) 99
Daily Meditation Practice (20-30 minutes) 101
Stage I: Focused Attention with Name and Form 101
Visual Summary: The Three Levels of Mind 104

MODULE 11: Power-Seeking, Mental Wandering, and Divine Providence 105
Daily Reflection Practice 105
Daily Contemplation Practice (15-20 minutes) 107
Daily Meditation Practice (20-30 minutes) 109
Stage Overview 109
Visual Summary: The Three Levels of Mind 111

MODULE 12: Transforming Destiny Through Purification 112
Daily Reflection Practice 112
Daily Contemplation Practice (15-20 minutes) 114
Daily Meditation Practice (20-30 minutes) 116

Stage Overview 116

Visual Summary: The Three Levels of Mind 118

MODULE 13: Commentary on Chapter 7B 119

Daily Reflection Practice 119

Daily Contemplation Practice (15-20 minutes) 121

Daily Meditation Practice (20-30 minutes) 123

Stage Overview 123

Visual Summary: The Three Levels of Mind 125

MODULE 14: The Serpent Power of Righteousness 126

Daily Reflection Practice 126

Daily Contemplation Practice (15-20 minutes) 128

Daily Meditation Practice (20-30 minutes) 130

Stage Overview 130

Visual Summary: The Three Levels of Mind 132

MODULE 15: Speech, Vitality, and the Path to Inner Sanctuary 133

Daily Reflection Practice 133

Daily Contemplation Practice (15-20 minutes) 135

Daily Meditation Practice (20-30 minutes) 136

Stage Overview 136

Visual Summary: The Three Levels of Mind 138

MODULE 16: Avoiding Heated Persons - Self-Control and Compassion 139

Understanding Your Journey to This Point 139

Daily Reflection Practice 141

THE GENTLE RETURN: Working with Mind Wandering During Practice 142

Daily Contemplation Practice (15-20 minutes) 145

Daily Meditation Practice (30-45 minutes) 147

LESSON 1: Breath Awareness with Gentle Return 147

Visual Summary: The Three Levels of Mind 151

MODULE 17: The Corruption of Greed and False Oaths 152

Daily Reflection Practice 152

Daily Contemplation Practice (15-20 minutes) 154

Daily Meditation Practice (30-45 minutes) 156

LESSON 2: Sound Awareness with Gentle Return 156

    Visual Summary: The Three Levels of Mind 159
  MODULE 18: The Complete Model of Mind and Consciousness - SYNTHESIS 160
    Daily Reflection Practice 160
    Daily Contemplation Practice (15-20 minutes) 162
    Daily Meditation Practice (30-45 minutes) 164
    LESSON 3: Visual Object (Apple) with Gentle Return 164
    Visual Summary: The Three Levels of Mind 167
  MODULE 19: The Glorification of Love Versus the Illusion of Power 168
    Daily Reflection Practice 168
    Daily Contemplation Practice (15-20 minutes) 170
    Daily Meditation Practice (30-45 minutes) 172
    LESSON 4: Body Sensation with Gentle Return 172
    Visual Summary: The Three Levels of Mind 175
  MODULE 20: The All-Seeing Eye of Cosmic Mind 176
    Daily Reflection Practice 176
    Daily Contemplation Practice (15-20 minutes) 178
    Daily Meditation Practice (30-45 minutes) 180
    LESSON 5: Thought Observation with Gentle Return 180
    Visual Summary: The Three Levels of Mind 183
  MODULE 21: The Psychology of Luxury Attachment 184
    Daily Reflection Practice 184
    Daily Contemplation Practice (15-20 minutes) 186
    Daily Meditation Practice (30-45 minutes) 188
    LESSON 6: Recognition of the Witness Itself 188
    Visual Summary: The Three Levels of Mind 191
  MODULE 22: The Psychology of Volitional Fraud 192
    Daily Reflection Practice 192
    Daily Contemplation Practice (15-20 minutes) 194
    Daily Meditation Practice (30-45 minutes) 196
    LESSON 7: Gap Extension Between Thoughts 196
    Visual Summary: The Three Levels of Mind 199
  MODULE 23: The Illusion of Self-Will and Divine Guidance 200
    Daily Reflection Practice 200

- Daily Contemplation Practice (15-20 minutes) 202
- Daily Meditation Practice (30-45 minutes) 204
- LESSON 8: Awareness Independent of Objects 204
- Visual Summary: The Three Levels of Mind 207

MODULE 24: Balance Between Trust and Righteous Action 208
- Daily Reflection Practice 208
- Daily Contemplation Practice (15-20 minutes) 210
- Daily Meditation Practice (30-45 minutes) 212
- LESSON 9: Prolonged Ab-Neter Recognition 212
- Visual Summary: The Three Levels of Mind 215

MODULE 25: Compassionate Treatment of the Vulnerable 216
- Daily Reflection Practice 216
- Daily Contemplation Practice (15-20 minutes) 218
- Daily Meditation Practice (45-60 minutes) 220
- LESSON 10 PARTS A-C: Daily Life Integration 220
- Visual Summary: The Three Levels of Mind 223

MODULE 26: The Path from Humility to Vigilant Serenity 224
- Daily Reflection Practice 224
- Daily Contemplation Practice (15-20 minutes) 226
- Daily Meditation Practice (45-60 minutes) 228
- LESSON 10 PARTS D-E: Advanced Integration & Path Completion 228
- PATH COMPLETION REFLECTION 229

HOW TO USE THIS WORKBOOK

This guidebook is designed as a companion to Dr. Muata Ashby's book, *Mental Health and Ancient Egyptian Psychology*, on the wisdom teachings of Sage Amenemopet. It provides structured practices, reflection exercises, and meditation instructions to help you integrate these profound teachings into your daily life and consciousness.

The Module System

This workbook contains 26 modules, each corresponding to a chapter commentary from the main text. Unlike traditional weekly programs, we use the term 'MODULE' to honor the truth that spiritual transformation occurs at its own natural pace—not according to predetermined schedules.

Important Understanding: Do not rush through modules. Spend as much time as needed with each teaching until you feel ready to move forward. Some practitioners may complete a module in a week; others may spend several weeks or even months with challenging teachings. Both approaches are valid and appropriate.

The Practice Progression

This guidebook guides you through a systematic progression:

- Modules 1-8: Contemplation Phase - Building capacity while learning philosophy (15-20 minutes daily)
- Module 9: Sau-Neberdjer Introduction - The pivotal transition to formal meditation practice
- Modules 10-15: Progressive Meditation Stages - Developing witness consciousness (20-30 minutes)
- Modules 16-26: Gentle Return Practice - Stabilization and daily life integration (30-45+ minutes)

Key Terms You'll Encounter

- **Hat: Conscious awareness - what is presently in your mind**
- **Ka: Subconscious mind and personality structure**
- **Ab: Unconscious mind - storehouse of aryu**
- **Aryu: Unconscious impressions/karmic patterns driving reactions**
- **Kara: Divine sanctuary within the ab where Ab Neter resides**
- **Ab Neter: Divine Heart/Divine Soul - your portion of divine consciousness**
- **Neberdjer: All-Encompassing Divinity - universal consciousness**
- **Udja: Vital-life-fire that purifies by burning away aryu density**
- **Shemm (Heated Person): Reactive, agitated consciousness dominated by aryu**

- **Ger (Silent Person): Peaceful, wise consciousness operating from divine awareness**
- **Maat: Truth, cosmic order, righteousness**
- **Sau-Neberdjer: Awareness-Meditation on the Absolute transcendental being of God – practice**
- **Sekhem: vital life-force / subtle vital body**

Important Recognition:

Working through all 26 modules does not mean you have mastered all the stages of consciousness transformation described. Rather, this guidebook helps your understanding of the stages while your actual realization develops through patient practice at its own pace. Meet yourself where you are, practice with sincerity, and trust the process.

Images of Sage Amenemopet:

Instructions of Amenemope, circa 12th century B.C.E. Ink on papyrus, British Museum, London.

The Wisdom Text Tradition and Spiritual Psychology

The Instructions of Amenemopet occupies a unique position within the corpus of Ancient Egyptian wisdom literature, bridging the earlier Pyramid Texts and Coffin Texts with the later developments of the Wasetian (Theban) tradition while maintaining its distinctive focus on practical psychological transformation [3]. This text belongs to the early and Middle Kingdom era, written during a period when the ancient sages had developed sophisticated understanding of consciousness levels and the precise mechanisms through which awareness becomes either trapped in ego-identification or liberated into recognition of its divine source [2][3]. Indeed, the teachings reveal that Amenemopet possessed profound insight into psychology and mysticism as well as what contemporary understanding might term transpersonal psychology—the systematic study of consciousness beyond the limitations of ego-based thinking and the practical methods for achieving expanded awareness that recognizes its essential unity with universal divine consciousness [4].

The sage's approach demonstrates remarkable sophistication in addressing what the ancient teachings identify as the fundamental human predicament: the tendency of consciousness to forget its divine nature and become trapped in cycles of seeking fulfillment through external means, creating what Amenemopet describes as the condition of the "heated person" (shemm) who lives through "unrighteousness, fraud, anger, boisterousness, flippant retorts and thoughtless speech, inconsiderate and impulsive acts, rapacious greed, jealousy, envy" [4]. This heated condition represents consciousness that has lost touch with its divine source and operates through accumulated aryu (karmic impressions) that cloud natural spiritual sensitivity and perpetuate endless cycles of dissatisfaction and suffering [4].

Consider how this understanding provides the essential framework for comprehending why practical spiritual development proves necessary and how it operates to transform consciousness from ego-identification to what the traditions call the Soul-Aware-Witness—that mode of awareness which has achieved separation from reactive patterns and now operates as the instrument of divine wisdom rather than the vehicle of worldly agitation [4]. The ancient sages taught that this transformation occurs through systematic cultivation of what Amenemopet terms the "silent mind" (ger), which discovers "the fullness of the Creator-Spirit that is within" rather than seeking satisfaction through heated engagement with worldly phenomena [4].

It bears emphasis that the term *ger* (silent) refers not to physical quietness or mere absence of speech, but rather to a **serene**, **balanced**, and **relaxed** quality of mind—the natural mental peace that emerges when consciousness no longer operates through the agitated patterns of heated thinking. The teaching's central focus concerns the practical methods for causing the mind to achieve and sustain this serenity, which represents the psychological foundation for discovering one's divine nature. In this context, the heated mind is usually considered "normal" by most people, however, the silent (serene) mind is to be considered the natural state. So, being "normal" is not always to be considered as good or healthy. Thus, the silent (serene) mind is a gateway to discovering deeper experiences of expanded consciousness.

MODULE 1: The Foundation of Wisdom Philosophy for Life Transformation

Difficulty Level: Foundational

Commentary on Amenemopet Prologue (verses 1-2, 7-9)

Life Vitality Health

Quick Chapter Overview

Key Teaching: The Prologue establishes the complete framework for Amenemopet's wisdom philosophy, revealing two interconnected goals: (1) achieving well-being while living on earth through developing vital-life-fire (udja) that produces spiritual purity, and (2) discovering the kara—the divine sanctuary where Ab Neter (divine soul) resides within every person.

Main Principles:

- Wisdom philosophy must be experienced through lived practice, not merely studied intellectually
- Precise understanding of spiritual teachings produces measurable well-being during earthly existence
- The ab (unconscious mind) has dual nature: it stores aryu (feeling memories) and contains Ab Neter (divine spark)
- Aryu density in the ab obscures awareness of Ab Neter, leaving consciousness aware only of body and mind
- The kara is the divine sanctuary where Ab Neter resides, revealed when aryu thin through purification
- When Ab Neter awareness is achieved, egoic impulses of aryu become powerless
- All personality desires are fulfilled when Ab Neter is discovered as the very nature of one's being

Daily Reflection Practice

Choose a verse from the Prologue to work with each day (verses 1, 2, 7, 8, or 9).

Read Dr. Ashby's translation and commentary carefully. Then write your reflections about what this teaching means in your life today. How does it expose aryu patterns? What resistance arises? Where do you see this teaching reflected in your daily experiences?

Reflection 1

Date: _____ Verse: _____

My reflections:

_____

_____

_____

Reflection 2

Date: _____ Verse: _____

My reflections:

_____

_____

_____

Reflection 3

Date: _____ Verse: _____

My reflections:

_____

_____

_____

Daily Contemplation Practice

After your written reflection, sit in contemplation with a focus phrase from this module's teachings.

Having practiced reflection, now sit while holding the meaning of the focus phrase from this module's teaching. Holding is not continuing to reflect, or think about it. Rather it means staying with the take-away meaning of the teaching for extended period. You have already reflected; now stay with the meaning as you understand it currently; what is the conclusion that the phrases brings you to?-this final conclusion/destination that the phrase has bought you to, is the focus for contemplation. If the mind wanders simply bring it back to the take-away objective of the focus phrase.

Focus Phrases for Contemplation:
- I place wisdom in my heart to transform consciousness
- Divine consciousness (Ab Neter) awakens in my inner sanctuary (kara)
- I witness my aryu patterns with compassion
- Wisdom descends from hat (mind) to ab (heart) through patient absorption
- Vital-life-fire (udja) burns away aryu density
- Ab Neter reveals itself when aryu thin through practice

Practice Instructions (15-20 minutes):

1. Choose a focus phrase from the list above

2. Sit comfortably with spine naturally erect, hands resting in lap

3. Close your eyes or maintain soft downward gaze

4. Bring attention to your heart center

5. Recall the take-away meaning from your reflection on this teaching

6. Hold this meaning without further analysis or thinking about it

7. When mind wanders into thoughts, gently return to holding the meaning

8. Continue for 15-20 minutes

9. End with three deep breaths and moment of gratitude

Practice Log

Session 1

Date: _____ Duration: _____

Key insights or challenges:

_____

_____

Session 2

Date: _____ Duration: _____

Key insights or challenges:

_____

_____

Session 3

Date: _____ Duration: _____

Key insights or challenges:

_____

_____

Aryu Pattern Recognition Exercise

Use this space to identify unconscious patterns (aryu) that the Prologue's teaching exposes. The teaching reveals that aryu in your ab (unconscious) influence your conscious thoughts and feelings, blocking awareness of Ab Neter. Practice witnessing these patterns with compassion, not self-criticism.

Observe situations this week where you notice:

- Living without conscious direction (random living vs. organized wisdom)
- Seeking fulfillment through external achievements rather than inner Ab Neter discovery
- Intellectual understanding without lived application
- Aryu storms overwhelming your conscious mind when triggered
- Forgetting your divine nature (Ab Neter) during daily activities

Record specific examples with compassionate awareness:

Example 1:

Situation: _____

Aryu pattern I recognized: _____

Connection to teaching: _____

_____

_____

Reflect on if the way you handled the situation was within the guidelines of the teaching or if not how it could have been handled in line with the teachings:
_____

_____

_____

Example 2:

Situation: _____

Aryu pattern I recognized: _____

Connection to teaching: _____

_____

Reflect on if the way you handled the situation was within the guidelines of the teaching or if not how it could have been handled in line with the teachings:
_____

_____

_____

Example 3:

Situation: _____

Aryu pattern I recognized: _____

Connection to teaching: _____

_____

_____

Reflect on if the way you handled the situation was within the guidelines of the teaching or if not how it could have been handled in line with the teachings:
_____

_____

_____

Deep Reflection Questions

Return to these questions multiple times as your understanding deepens. Your answers may change as the teaching penetrates from intellectual comprehension (hat level) to heart-wisdom (ab level) and ignites udja (vital-life-fire).

Question 1: What is the difference between intellectual understanding of these teachings and having them 'experienced in life' as verse 1 instructs?

My response:

_____

_____

_____

Question 2: How does recognizing the dual goals (earthly well-being AND Ab Neter discovery) change my approach to spiritual practice?

My response:

_____

_____

_____

Question 3: What aryu patterns currently dominate my conscious awareness, blocking recognition of Ab Neter?

My response:

_____

_____

_____

Question 4: Where in my life am I seeking fulfillment through external means rather than discovering the divine foundation within (kara)?

My response:

_____

_____

_____

Question 5: How would my daily life transform if I truly recognized Ab Neter as the foundation sustaining my awareness?

My response:

_____

_____

_____

Visual Summary: The Three Levels of Mind

Draw or create a visual representation of how the wisdom you learned in this module relates in your own experience. Use any or all of the following: colors, symbols, hieroglyphs, codes, shapes, etc. in the open space below.

Module Completion Reflection

Before moving to Module 2, honestly assess your readiness. The Prologue establishes the foundation for all subsequent teachings—understanding these dual goals deeply is essential.

Signs of Readiness:

☐ I can articulate the two Prologue goals and their interconnection

☐ I understand the distinction between hat, ab, kara, and Ab Neter

☐ I recognize aryu patterns in my own consciousness without harsh self-judgment

☐ My contemplation practice with these focus phrases feels natural and stable

☐ I've noticed at least one shift in how I approach daily life through this wisdom

☐ I've practiced reflection and contemplation consistently with this module

Important: If you don't yet experience these signs, remain with Module 1 longer. The Prologue is the foundation for everything that follows. Transformation cannot be rushed.

Date completed: _____

What was the most significant insight you learned in this module from this module:

_____

_____

_____

_____

MODULE 2: The Psychology of Wisdom Absorption and Aryu Purification

Difficulty Level: ● Foundational

Commentary on Amenemopet Chapter 1, Verses 8-18 & 1-2

Life Vitality Health

Quick Chapter Overview

Key Teaching: This chapter addresses the critical distinction between superficial intellectual exposure to spiritual teachings and authentic deep absorption that ignites vital-life-fire (udja)—the purifying spiritual fire that transforms the mind by burning away aryu density and revealing Ab Neter awareness.

Main Principles:

- Superficial hearing differs fundamentally from deep listening that ignites vital-life-fire (udja)
- Wisdom teachings must be absorbed into 'the innermost levels of the mind (unconscious)' to activate purifying fire
- Aryu (karmic-feeling-memories) stored in ab arise into conscious awareness creating 'storming of words'
- Properly absorbed wisdom acts as 'mooring post' infused with vital-life-fire preventing mind from being swept away
- 'Living ears' represent mind genuinely ready for transformation through ignition of spiritual purifying fire
- Becoming 'remote in your mind, detached and collected' enables wisdom absorption that ignites udja
- The transformation process requires both conscious study and unconscious integration that ignites purifying fire

Daily Reflection Practice

Choose verses from Chapter 1 (verses 8-18, 1-2) to work with each day.

Read Dr. Ashby's translation and commentary carefully. Reflect on how these teachings expose the difference between surface learning and deep absorption. Where do you recognize superficial spiritual engagement in your life? What prevents teachings from penetrating to the unconscious level?

Reflection 1

Date: _____ Verse: _____

My reflections:

_____

_____

_____

Reflection 2

Date: _____ Verse: _____

My reflections:

_____

_____

_____

Reflection 3

Date: _____ Verse: _____

My reflections:

_____

_____

_____

Daily Contemplation Practice

After your written reflection, sit in contemplation with a focus phrase from this module's teachings.

Having practiced reflection, now sit while holding the meaning of the focus phrase from this module's teaching. Holding is not continuing to reflect, or think about it. Rather it means staying with the take-away meaning of the teaching for extended period. You have already reflected; now stay with the meaning as you understand it currently. If the mind wanders simply bring it back to the take-away objective of the focus phrase.

Focus Phrases for Contemplation:

- I allow wisdom to penetrate from hat (mind) to ab (heart) through patient absorption
- Vital-life-fire (udja) ignites when teachings reach innermost levels of mind
- I cultivate 'living ears' genuinely ready for transformation
- Wisdom acts as mooring post when aryu storms arise in consciousness
- I become remote in mind, detached and collected, to enable deep absorption
- The purifying fire burns away aryu density revealing Ab Neter awareness

Practice Instructions (15-20 minutes):

1. Choose a focus phrase from the list above

2. Sit comfortably with spine naturally erect, hands resting in lap

3. Close your eyes or maintain soft downward gaze

4. Bring attention to your heart center

5. Recall the take-away meaning from your reflection on this teaching

6. Hold this meaning without further analysis or thinking about it

7. When mind wanders into thoughts, gently return to holding the meaning

8. Continue for 15-20 minutes

9. End with three deep breaths and moment of gratitude

Practice Log
Session 1

Date: _____ Duration: _____

Key insights or challenges:

_____

_____

Session 2

Date: _____ Duration: _____

Key insights or challenges:

_____

_____

Session 3

Date: _____ Duration: _____

Key insights or challenges:

_____

_____

Aryu Pattern Recognition Exercise

Use this space to identify unconscious patterns (aryu) that this module's teaching exposes. Practice witnessing these patterns with compassion, not self-criticism.

Record specific examples with compassionate awareness:

Example 1:

Situation: _____

Aryu pattern I recognized: _____

Connection to teaching: _____

_____

_____

Reflect on if the way you handled the situation was within the guidelines of the teaching or if not how it could have been handled in line with the teachings:

_____

_____

_____

Example 2:

Situation: _____

Aryu pattern I recognized: _____

Connection to teaching: _____

_____

_____

Reflect on if the way you handled the situation was within the guidelines of the teaching or if not how it could have been handled in line with the teachings:

_____

_____

_____

Example 3:

Situation: _____

Aryu pattern I recognized: _____

Connection to teaching: _____

_____

_____

Reflect on if the way you handled the situation was within the guidelines of the teaching or if not how it could have been handled in line with the teachings:

_____

_____

_____

Deep Reflection Questions

Return to these questions multiple times as your understanding deepens. Your answers may change as the teaching penetrates from intellectual comprehension to heart-wisdom.

Question 1: What is the difference between intellectual understanding and wisdom that ignites vital-life-fire (udja)?

My response:

_____

_____

_____

Question 2: Where in my spiritual practice do I engage superficially rather than allowing deep absorption?

My response:

_____

_____

_____

Question 3: What aryu patterns create 'storming of words' when triggered, overwhelming my conscious mind?

My response:

_____

_____

_____

Question 4: How would developing 'living ears' change my approach to studying spiritual teachings?

My response:

_____

_____

_____

Question 5: What would it feel like if wisdom acted as a 'mooring post' when aryu storms arise?

My response:

_____

_____

_____

Visual Summary: The Three Levels of Mind

Draw or create a visual representation of how the wisdom you learned in this module relates in your own experience. Use any or all of the following: colors, symbols, hieroglyphs, codes, shapes, etc. in the open space below.

Module Completion Reflection

Before moving to the next module, honestly assess your readiness:

Signs of Readiness:

☐ I understand the distinction between superficial and deep wisdom absorption

☐ I can recognize when aryu create 'storming of words' in my consciousness

☐ I've identified specific areas where my spiritual engagement remains superficial

☐ My contemplation practice with these focus phrases feels natural

☐ I've noticed shifts in how teachings are affecting my mind

☐ I've practiced reflection and contemplation consistently with this module

Important: If you don't yet experience these signs, remain with this module longer. Transformation cannot be rushed.

Date completed: _____

What was the most significant insight you learned in this module from this module:

_____

_____

_____

_____

MODULE 3: The Cosmic Psychology of Unrighteous Action and the Enemy of Life

Difficulty Level: ◐ Foundational

Commentary on Amenemopet Chapter 2, Verses 10, 16-17

Life Vitality Health

Quick Chapter Overview

Key Teaching: This chapter reveals how unrighteous actions sever consciousness from the neteru (cosmic forces/gods and goddesses) commissioned by Neberdjer to care for Creation, creating both external chaos ('tempests in life with thunderousness') and internal vulnerability to unconscious patterns ('crocodiles lying in wait').

Main Principles:

- Bad actions according to Maat philosophy act as means of forsaking the caring of natural forces
- Unrighteous actions disconnect consciousness from neteru (gods/goddesses) that sustain well-being
- Coming out of harmony with nature develops personality into ragefulness, anger, and anxiety
- Heated condition (shemm) creates personality negative in disposition, feeling, and cognition
- Set symbolism represents egoistic foundation generating heated personality expressions
- Tempestuousness arises from ego (Set), not from Ab Neter or essential divine nature
- Heated person becomes 'enemy of life' through opposition to harmony with natural forces
- Life means being in physical and mental harmony with forces of nature (neteru)

Daily Reflection Practice

Choose verses from Chapter 2 (verses 10, 16-17) to work with each day.

Reflect on how unrighteous actions sever your connection with natural harmony. Where do you recognize patterns of turning away from the caring of natural forces? How does egoism (Set) create tempests in your life?

Reflection 1

Date: _____ Verse: _____

My reflections:

_____

_____

_____

Reflection 2

Date: _____ Verse: _____

My reflections:

_____

_____

_____

Reflection 3

Date: _____ Verse: _____

My reflections:

_____

_____

_____

Daily Contemplation Practice

After your written reflection, sit in contemplation with a focus phrase from this module's teachings.

Having practiced reflection, now sit while holding the meaning of the focus phrase from this module's teaching. Holding is not continuing to reflect, or think about it. Rather it means staying with the take-away meaning of the teaching for extended period. You have already reflected; now stay with the meaning as you understand it currently. If the mind wanders simply bring it back to the take-away objective of the focus phrase.

Focus Phrases for Contemplation:

- I maintain harmony with natural forces (neteru) through righteous action
- Egoism (Set) creates tempests; Ab Neter creates peace
- I witness crocodiles lying in wait in my unconscious without fear
- Life means harmony with forces of nature ordained by Neberdjer
- I turn from heated patterns toward silent communion with cosmic forces
- Unrighteousness severs divine connection; righteousness restores it

Practice Instructions (15-20 minutes):

1. Choose a focus phrase from the list above

2. Sit comfortably with spine naturally erect

3. Close your eyes or maintain soft downward gaze

4. Bring attention to your heart center

5. Recall the take-away meaning from your reflection

6. Hold this meaning without further analysis

7. When mind wanders, gently return to holding the meaning

8. Continue for 15-20 minutes

9. End with three deep breaths and gratitude

Practice Log

Session 1

Date: _____ Duration: _____

Key insights or challenges:

_____

_____

Session 2

Date: _____ Duration: _____

Key insights or challenges:

_____

_____

Session 3

Date: _____ Duration: _____

Key insights or challenges:

_____

_____

Session 4

Date: _____ Duration: _____

Key insights or challenges:

_____

_____

Session 5

Date: _____ Duration: _____

Key insights or challenges:

_____

_____

Aryu Pattern Recognition Exercise

Identify patterns where you forsake natural harmony through unrighteous action. Observe with compassion where egoism (Set) creates tempests in your life.

Example 1:

Situation: _____

Aryu pattern I recognized: _____

Connection to teaching: _____

_____

_____

Example 2:

Situation: _____

Aryu pattern I recognized: _____

Connection to teaching: _____

_____

_____

Example 3:

Situation: _____

Aryu pattern I recognized: _____

Connection to teaching: _____

_____

_____

Deep Reflection Questions

Return to these questions multiple times as understanding deepens.

Question 1: What specific actions sever my connection with the neteru (cosmic forces) that sustain well-being?

My response:

_____

_____

_____

Question 2: How does egoism (Set) create 'tempests with thunderousness' in my external and internal life?

My response:

_____

_____

_____

Question 3: What 'crocodiles lying in wait' in my unconscious mind strike unexpectedly when I act unrighteously?

My response:

_____

_____

_____

Question 4: How have I become an 'enemy of life' by opposing harmony with natural forces?

My response:

_____

_____

_____

Question 5: What would shift if I recognized that tempestuousness arises from ego, not from my divine nature (Ab Neter)?

My response:

_____

_____

_____

Visual Summary: The Three Levels of Mind

Draw or create a visual representation of how the wisdom you learned in this module relates in your own experience. Use any or all of the following: colors, symbols, hieroglyphs, codes, shapes, etc. in the open space below.

Module Completion Reflection

Before moving to Module 4, assess your readiness:

Signs of Readiness:

☐ I understand how unrighteous actions sever connection with cosmic forces

☐ I can identify Set (ego) patterns creating tempests in my life

☐ I recognize that tempestuousness arises from ego, not my divine nature

☐ I've noticed unconscious 'crocodiles' that strike when I act unrighteously

☐ My contemplation practice feels grounded and natural

☐ I've practiced consistently with this module

Important: Remain with this module until these understandings stabilize.

Date completed: _____

What was the most significant insight you learned in this module from this module:

_____
_____
_____
_____

MODULE 4: The Sacred Navigation of Life's Journey - Conscious Effort

Difficulty Level: 🌑 Foundational

Commentary on Amenemopet Chapter 2V, Verses 1-2

Ankh Udja Senab
Life Vitality Health

Quick Chapter Overview

Key Teaching: This chapter teaches the necessity of conscious effort to steer the boat of life away from what is bad. The metaphor reveals that spiritual development requires active navigation—applying force/effort to turn around and go another way rather than drifting toward heated patterns.

Main Principles:

- The boat of life requires conscious steering through applied effort
- One must actively steer away from bad actions and heated persons
- Turning around means choosing different direction rather than joining heated doings
- Conscious effort prevents drifting into unrighteous patterns
- Navigation requires constant vigilance and willful redirection
- Spiritual progress demands active choice, not passive acceptance

Daily Reflection Practice

Work with Chapter 2V verses 1-2 each day.

Reflect on the metaphor of steering your boat of life. Where do you drift toward heated patterns without conscious effort? What would it mean to actively 'turn around and go another way'?

Reflection 1

Date: _____ Verse: _____

My reflections:

_____

_____

_____

Reflection 2

Date: _____ Verse: _____

My reflections:

_____

_____

_____

Reflection 3

Date: _____ Verse: _____

My reflections:

_____

_____

_____

Daily Contemplation Practice

After your written reflection, sit in contemplation with a focus phrase from this module's teachings.

Having practiced reflection, now sit while holding the meaning of the focus phrase from this module's teaching. Holding is not continuing to reflect, or think about it. Rather it means staying with the take-away meaning of the teaching for extended period. You have already reflected; now stay with the meaning as you understand it currently. If the mind wanders simply bring it back to the take-away objective of the focus phrase.

Focus Phrases for Contemplation:
- I consciously steer my boat of life away from what is bad
- I apply effort to turn around rather than join heated doings
- Navigation requires vigilance; I do not drift into unrighteousness
- I actively choose silent path over heated patterns
- My life journey demands conscious effort, not passive drift
- I recognize when to turn around and go another way

Practice Instructions (15-20 minutes):

1. Choose a focus phrase from the list above

2. Sit comfortably with spine naturally erect

3. Close your eyes or maintain soft downward gaze

4. Bring attention to your heart center

5. Recall the take-away meaning from your reflection

6. Hold this meaning without further analysis

7. When mind wanders, gently return to holding the meaning

8. Continue for 15-20 minutes

9. End with three deep breaths and gratitude

Practice Log
Session 1

Date: _____ Duration: _____

Key insights or challenges:

_____

_____

Session 2

Date: _____ Duration: _____

Key insights or challenges:

_____

_____

Session 3

Date: _____ Duration: _____

Key insights or challenges:

_____

_____

Session 4

Date: _____ Duration: _____

Key insights or challenges:

_____

_____

Session 5

Date: _____ Duration: _____

Key insights or challenges:

_____

_____

Aryu Pattern Recognition Exercise

Identify areas where you drift toward heated patterns without conscious navigation. Where have you failed to apply effort to steer away from what is bad?

Example 1:

Situation: _____

Aryu pattern I recognized: _____

Connection to teaching: _____

_____

_____

Example 2:

Situation: _____

Aryu pattern I recognized: _____

Connection to teaching: _____

_____

_____

Example 3:

Situation: _____

Aryu pattern I recognized: _____

Connection to teaching: _____

_____

_____

Deep Reflection Questions

Question 1: Where in my life do I drift toward heated patterns without conscious steering?

My response:

_____

_____

_____

Question 2: What would it require to 'apply force/effort' to steer away from what is bad?

My response:

_____

_____

_____

Question 3: How do I distinguish between passive acceptance and active spiritual navigation?

My response:

_____

_____

_____

Question 4: What heated patterns require me to 'turn around and go another way'?

My response:

_____

_____

_____

Question 5: What resistance arises when I consider applying conscious effort to redirect my life's journey?

My response:

_____

_____

_____

Module Completion Reflection

Signs of Readiness:

☐ I understand the necessity of conscious effort in spiritual development

☐ I can identify areas where I drift rather than actively navigate

☐ I recognize what it means to 'turn around and go another way'

☐ I've applied conscious steering in at least one area of life

☐ My contemplation practice feels integrated

☐ I've practiced consistently with this module

Date completed: _____

What was the most significant insight you learned in this module:

_____

_____

_____

_____

MODULE 5: The Sacred Art of Spiritual Discernment - Conscious Disassociation

Difficulty Level: Foundational

Commentary on Amenemopet Chapter 3, Verses 10, 15-17

Ankh Udja Senab
Life Vitality Health

Quick Chapter Overview

Key Teaching: This chapter teaches the essential skill of conscious disassociation from heated mind and feelings—whether in others or arising within oneself. The wisdom reveals how prolonged association with heated patterns activates similar patterns in one's own consciousness, making conscious mental redirection necessary for spiritual protection.

Main Principles:

- Desist from joining with, gossiping with, or arguing with heated persons (the 'sneaky enemy')
- During someone's 'time of intense heat,' reject them by turning your mind away from their mind and emotions
- Heated persons are misleading personalities who lead others away from silent path
- Turn your mind away without concern for their fate—Divine will provide what they need
- Heated mind and feelings is contagious; prolonged association activates similar patterns in your consciousness
- The 'internal sneaky enemy' operates through willful ignorance and self-deceptive rationalization
- Conscious disassociation applies equally to external heated persons and one's own egoic patterns

Daily Reflection Practice

Choose verses from this chapter to work with each day.

Reflect on situations where you engage with heated persons or patterns. Where does association with heated energy activate similar patterns in your consciousness? How might conscious disassociation serve your spiritual development?

Reflection 1

Date: _____ Verse: _____

My reflections:

_____

_____

_____

Reflection 2

Date: _____ Verse: _____

My reflections:

_____

_____

_____

Reflection 3

Date: _____ Verse: _____

My reflections:

_____

_____

_____

Daily Contemplation Practice

After your written reflection, sit in contemplation with a focus phrase from this module's teachings.

Having practiced reflection, now sit while holding the meaning of the focus phrase from this module's teaching. Holding is not continuing to reflect, or think about it. Rather it means staying with the take-away meaning of the teaching for extended period. You have already reflected; now stay with the meaning as you understand it currently. If the mind wanders simply bring it back to the take-away objective of the focus phrase.

Focus Phrases for Contemplation:

- I consciously disassociate from heated mind and feelings to protect my spiritual development
- I turn my mind away from heated patterns without guilt or concern
- Divine providence handles those from whom I maintain distance
- I recognize the internal sneaky enemy operating through rationalization
- I maintain silent path by avoiding engagement with heated consciousness
- Conscious disassociation is spiritual protection, not lack of compassion

Practice Instructions (15-20 minutes):

1. Choose a focus phrase from the list above

2. Sit comfortably with spine naturally erect

3. Close your eyes or maintain soft downward gaze

4. Bring attention to your heart center

5. Recall the take-away meaning from your reflection

6. Hold this meaning without further analysis

7. When mind wanders, gently return to holding the meaning

8. Continue for 15-20 minutes

9. End with three deep breaths and gratitude

Practice Log

Session 1

Date: _____ Duration: _____

Key insights or challenges:

_____

_____

Session 2

Date: _____ Duration: _____

Key insights or challenges:

_____

_____

Session 3

Date: _____ Duration: _____

Key insights or challenges:

_____

_____

Session 4

Date: _____ Duration: _____

Key insights or challenges:

_____

_____

Session 5

Date: _____ Duration: _____

Key insights or challenges:

_____

_____

Aryu Pattern Recognition Exercise

Identify patterns that this module's teaching exposes. Observe with compassion.

Example 1:

Situation: _____

Aryu pattern I recognized: _____

Connection to teaching: _____

_____

_____

Example 2:

Situation: _____

Aryu pattern I recognized: _____

Connection to teaching: _____

_____

_____

Example 3:

Situation: _____

Aryu pattern I recognized: _____

Connection to teaching: _____

_____

_____

Deep Reflection Questions

Return to these questions multiple times as understanding deepens.

Question 1: Where do I engage with heated persons in ways that activate heated patterns in my own consciousness?

My response:

_____

_____

_____

Question 2: How do I distinguish between compassionate engagement and heated entanglement?

My response:

_____

_____

_____

Question 3: What 'internal sneaky enemy' patterns use spiritual rationalizations to justify unrighteous behavior?

My response:

_____

_____

_____

Question 4: What resistance arises when I consider turning my mind away from heated situations?

My response:

_____

_____

Question 5: How would my spiritual development change if I practiced consistent conscious disassociation?

My response:

Visual Summary: The Three Levels of Mind

Draw or create a visual representation of how the wisdom you learned in this module relates in your own experience. Use any or all of the following: colors, symbols, hieroglyphs, codes, shapes, etc. in the open space below.

Module Completion Reflection

Before moving to the next module, assess your readiness:

Signs of Readiness:

☐ I understand the contagious nature of heated mind and feelings

☐ I can identify when to turn my mind away from heated patterns

☐ I recognize the internal sneaky enemy operating through rationalization

☐ I've practiced conscious disassociation in at least one situation

☐ My contemplation practice feels integrated

☐ I've practiced consistently with this module

Important: Remain with this module until these understandings stabilize.

Date completed: _____

What was the most significant insight you learned in this module:

_____
_____
_____

MODULE 6: The Psychology of Spiritual Receptivity and Silent Mind and Feelings

Commentary on Amenemopet Chapter 4, Verses 1-2, 7-8

Life Vitality Health

Quick Chapter Overview

Key Teaching: This chapter reveals the psychological distinction between heated and silent persons approaching spiritual teachings. Like trees in the temple but receiving no sun or rain benefit, heated persons remain unreceptive to divine illumination even in sacred space. Silent persons demonstrate the receptivity necessary for spiritual transformation.

Main Principles:

- Heated persons entering temple are like trees in a covered building—receiving no illumination
- Even in sacred space, heated aryu patterns prevent reception of divine teaching
- Silent person (ger) demonstrates receptivity through detached, collected mind
- Silent mind and feelings create conditions for spiritual benefits to penetrate consciousness
- The distinction between heated and silent persons determines spiritual receptivity
- Transformation requires not merely exposure to teachings but inner preparation to receive them
- Silence cultivated through practice creates the receptivity necessary for divine illumination

Daily Reflection Practice

Choose verses from this chapter to work with each day.

Reflect on your receptivity to spiritual teachings. Are there areas where you approach spiritual practice like heated person entering temple—present physically but unreceptive inwardly? How might cultivating silent mind and feelings increase your spiritual receptivity?

Reflection 1

Date: _____ Verse: _____

My reflections:

_____

_____

_____

Reflection 2

Date: _____ Verse: _____

My reflections:

_____

_____

_____

Reflection 3

Date: _____ Verse: _____

My reflections:

_____

_____

_____

Daily Contemplation Practice

After your written reflection, sit in contemplation with a focus phrase from this module's teachings.

Having practiced reflection, now sit while holding the meaning of the focus phrase from this module's teaching. Holding is not continuing to reflect, or think about it. Rather it means staying with the take-away meaning of the teaching for extended period. You have already reflected; now stay with the meaning as you understand it currently. If the mind wanders simply bring it back to the take-away objective of the focus phrase.

Focus Phrases for Contemplation:

- I cultivate silent mind and feelings (ger) to receive divine illumination
- I recognize when heated patterns block spiritual receptivity
- Like a tree in sunlight, I position consciousness to receive divine teaching
- Silence creates receptivity; agitation creates obstruction
- I prepare inner sanctuary to receive wisdom's transforming power
- Spiritual benefit depends on receptivity, not mere exposure to teachings

Practice Instructions (15-20 minutes):

1. Choose a focus phrase from the list above

2. Sit comfortably with spine naturally erect

3. Close your eyes or maintain soft downward gaze

4. Bring attention to your heart center

5. Recall the take-away meaning from your reflection

6. Hold this meaning without further analysis

7. When mind wanders, gently return to holding the meaning

8. Continue for 15-20 minutes

9. End with three deep breaths and gratitude

Practice Log
Session 1

Date: _____ Duration: _____

Key insights or challenges:

_____

_____

Session 2

Date: _____ Duration: _____

Key insights or challenges:

_____

_____

Session 3

Date: _____ Duration: _____

Key insights or challenges:

_____

_____

Session 4

Date: _____ Duration: _____

Key insights or challenges:

_____

_____

Session 5

Date: _____ Duration: _____

Key insights or challenges:

_____

_____

Aryu Pattern Recognition Exercise

Identify patterns that this module's teaching exposes. Observe with compassion.

Example 1:

Situation: _____

Aryu pattern I recognized: _____

Connection to teaching: _____

_____

_____

Example 2:

Situation: _____

Aryu pattern I recognized: _____

Connection to teaching: _____

_____

_____

Example 3:

Situation: _____

Aryu pattern I recognized: _____

Connection to teaching: _____

_____

_____

Deep Reflection Questions

Return to these questions multiple times as understanding deepens.

Question 1: In what ways do I approach spiritual teachings like 'a tree in a covered building'—present but unreceptive?

My response:

_____

_____

_____

Question 2: What heated patterns obstruct my receptivity even when I'm exposed to authentic teachings?

My response:

_____

_____

_____

Question 3: How can I cultivate the silent mind and feelings (ger) that creates genuine receptivity?

My response:

_____

_____

_____

Question 4: What is the difference between intellectual exposure and spiritual reception of teachings?

My response:

_____

_____

Question 5: How would my spiritual development accelerate if I cultivated greater receptivity?

My response:

Visual Summary: The Three Levels of Mind

Draw or create a visual representation of how the wisdom you learned in this module relates in your own experience. Use any or all of the following: colors, symbols, hieroglyphs, codes, shapes, etc. in the open space below.

Module Completion Reflection

Before moving to the next module, assess your readiness:

Signs of Readiness:

☐ I understand the difference between exposure and receptivity to spiritual teachings

☐ I can identify heated patterns that obstruct spiritual reception

☐ I recognize characteristics of silent mind and feelings (ger)

☐ I've cultivated greater receptivity in my spiritual practice

☐ My contemplation practice demonstrates increasing stillness

☐ I've practiced consistently with this module

Important: Remain with this module until these understandings stabilize.

Date completed: _____

What was the most significant insight you learned in this module:

_____

_____

_____

MODULE 7: The Psychology of Inner Fulfillment Through Divine Communion

Difficulty Level: Intermediate

Commentary on Amenemopet Chapter 5, Verses 7-9

Life Vitality Health

Quick Chapter Overview

Key Teaching: This chapter addresses the fundamental drive for fulfillment that characterizes human consciousness. The teaching reveals that all external seeking arises from felt incompleteness, and true fulfillment comes through communion with Creator-Spirit within rather than acquisition of worldly experiences.

Main Principles:

- Silent persons entering temple speak of blessings received from Creator-Spirit
- Being silent means discovering fullness of Creator-Spirit within through communion
- Heated search for fulfillment in world with imperfect personality proves futile
- True fulfillment comes from recognizing perfection within when fullness is experienced beyond worldly cravings
- External seeking arises from egoic sense of incompleteness and separation
- Communion with Creator-Spirit in temple (kara) provides authentic satisfaction
- All personality desires are fulfilled when Ab Neter is discovered as the very nature of one's being

Daily Reflection Practice

Choose verses from this chapter to work with each day.

Reflect on your seeking patterns. Where do you search for fulfillment through external means—relationships, achievements, possessions, experiences? How might turning attention inward toward communion with Creator-Spirit provide the completion you seek?

Reflection 1

Date: _____ Verse: _____

My reflections:

_____

_____

_____

Reflection 2

Date: _____ Verse: _____

My reflections:

_____

_____

_____

Reflection 3

Date: _____ Verse: _____

My reflections:

_____

_____

_____

Daily Contemplation Practice

After your written reflection, sit in contemplation with a focus phrase from this module's teachings.

Having practiced reflection, now sit while holding the meaning of the focus phrase from this module's teaching. Holding is not continuing to reflect, or think about it. Rather it means staying with the take-away meaning of the teaching for extended period. You have already reflected; now stay with the meaning as you understand it currently. If the mind wanders simply bring it back to the take-away objective of the focus phrase.

Focus Phrases for Contemplation:

- I discover fullness of Creator-Spirit within through silent communion
- I recognize that external seeking arises from felt incompleteness
- True fulfillment comes from communion with divine presence in kara
- Worldly satisfaction proves ephemeral; divine communion provides perennial completeness
- I am already complete through Ab Neter; I seek externally through ignorance
- Silent approach reveals the fullness I sought was always within

Practice Instructions (15-20 minutes):

1. Choose a focus phrase from the list above

2. Sit comfortably with spine naturally erect

3. Close your eyes or maintain soft downward gaze

4. Bring attention to your heart center

5. Recall the take-away meaning from your reflection

6. Hold this meaning without further analysis

7. When mind wanders, gently return to holding the meaning

8. Continue for 15-20 minutes

9. End with three deep breaths and gratitude

Practice Log

Session 1

Date: _____ Duration: _____

Key insights or challenges:

_____

Session 2

Date: _____ Duration: _____

Key insights or challenges:

_____

_____

Session 3

Date: _____ Duration: _____

Key insights or challenges:

_____

_____

Session 4

Date: _____ Duration: _____

Key insights or challenges:

_____

_____

Session 5

Date: _____ Duration: _____

Key insights or challenges:

_____

_____

Aryu Pattern Recognition Exercise

Identify patterns that this module's teaching exposes. Observe with compassion.

Example 1:

Situation: _____

Aryu pattern I recognized: _____

Connection to teaching: _____

_____

_____

Example 2:

Situation: _____

Aryu pattern I recognized: _____

Connection to teaching: _____

_____

_____

Example 3:

Situation: _____

Aryu pattern I recognized: _____

Connection to teaching: _____

_____

_____

Deep Reflection Questions

Return to these questions multiple times as understanding deepens.

Question 1: Where do I seek fulfillment through external acquisition rather than internal communion?

My response:

_____

_____

_____

Question 2: What felt incompleteness drives my egoic seeking in the world?

My response:

_____

_____

_____

Question 3: How have my attempts at worldly fulfillment proven ephemeral and unsatisfying?

My response:

_____

_____

_____

Question 4: What would shift if I recognized that true completion comes through discovering Creator-Spirit within?

My response:

_____

_____

Question 5: How can I cultivate the silent approach that enables communion with divine presence in kara?

My response:

Visual Summary: The Three Levels of Mind

Draw or create a visual representation of how the wisdom you learned in this module relates in your own experience. Use any or all of the following: colors, symbols, hieroglyphs, codes, shapes, etc. in the open space below.

Module Completion Reflection

Before moving to the next module, assess your readiness:

Signs of Readiness:

☐ I understand that external seeking arises from felt incompleteness

☐ I recognize how worldly fulfillment proves ephemeral

☐ I've experienced moments of inner communion beyond external seeking

☐ I can identify the silent approach that enables divine communion

☐ My contemplation practice reveals growing inner fulfillment

☐ I've practiced consistently with this module

Important: Remain with this module until these understandings stabilize.

Date completed: _____

What was the most significant insight you learned in this module:

_____

_____

_____

_____

MODULE 8: Maintaining Awareness of All-Encompassing Divinity - Deliberate Neberdjer Recognition

Commentary on Amenemopet Chapter 6B, Verse 14

Ankh Udja Senab
Life Vitality Health

Quick Chapter Overview

Key Teaching: This pivotal verse introduces Sau-Neberdjer—the practice of maintaining awareness of the All-Encompassing Divinity (Neberdjer) underlying all Creation. The teaching instructs: 'Remain aware, with deliberate effort, as to the fact that there is an existence that encompasses all Creation, beyond mind and time and space.'

Main Principles:

- Neberdjer is All-Encompassing Divinity, Lord of utmost limits
- This existence/consciousness underlies and encompasses all limited human awareness
- Awareness of Neberdjer must be maintained with deliberate effort and conscious volition
- This practice represents preparation for formal meditation (Sau-Neberdjer)
- Maintaining Neberdjer awareness throughout daily activities transforms consciousness
- The teaching establishes six progressive dimensions of Sau-Neberdjer practice
- This awareness must be maintained above all else as primary spiritual practice

Daily Reflection Practice

Choose verses from this chapter to work with each day.

Reflect on the instruction to maintain awareness of Neberdjer 'with deliberate effort.' How might this practice transform your daily experience? What challenges arise when attempting to maintain this awareness throughout activities?

Reflection 1

Date: _____ Verse: _____

My reflections:

_____

_____

_____

Reflection 2

Date: _____ Verse: _____

My reflections:

_____

_____

_____

Reflection 3

Date: _____ Verse: _____

My reflections:

_____

_____

_____

Daily Contemplation Practice

After your written reflection, sit in contemplation with a focus phrase from this module's teachings.

Having practiced reflection, now sit while holding the meaning of the focus phrase from this module's teaching. Holding is not continuing to reflect, or think about it. Rather it means staying with the take-away meaning of the teaching for extended period. You have already reflected; now stay with the meaning as you understand it currently. If the mind wanders simply bring it back to the take-away objective of the focus phrase.

Focus Phrases for Contemplation:

- I remain aware of Neberdjer—the All-Encompassing Divinity—with deliberate effort
- All Creation exists within and as Neberdjer; nothing exists outside this consciousness
- My limited awareness operates within the infinite awareness of Neberdjer
- I maintain this awareness above all else throughout daily activities
- Neberdjer is the consciousness underlying mind, time, and space
- I prepare for formal meditation by cultivating this deliberate recognition

Practice Instructions (15-20 minutes):

1. Choose a focus phrase from the list above

2. Sit comfortably with spine naturally erect

3. Close your eyes or maintain soft downward gaze

4. Bring attention to your heart center

5. Recall the take-away meaning from your reflection

6. Hold this meaning without further analysis

7. When mind wanders, gently return to holding the meaning

8. Continue for 15-20 minutes

9. End with three deep breaths and gratitude

Practice Log

Session 1

Date: _____ Duration: _____

Key insights or challenges:

_____

_____

Session 2

Date: _____ Duration: _____

Key insights or challenges:

_____

_____

Session 3

Date: _____ Duration: _____

Key insights or challenges:

_____

_____

Session 4

Date: _____ Duration: _____

Key insights or challenges:

_____

_____

Session 5

Date: _____ Duration: _____

Key insights or challenges:

_____

_____

Aryu Pattern Recognition Exercise

Identify patterns that this module's teaching exposes. Observe with compassion.

Example 1:

Situation: _____

Aryu pattern I recognized: _____

Connection to teaching: _____

_____

_____

Example 2:

Situation: _____

Aryu pattern I recognized: _____

Connection to teaching: _____

_____

_____

Example 3:

Situation: _____

Aryu pattern I recognized: _____

Connection to teaching: _____

_____

_____

Deep Reflection Questions

Return to these questions multiple times as understanding deepens.

Question 1: What does it mean practically to 'remain aware of Neberdjer with deliberate effort'?

My response:

_____

_____

_____

Question 2: How is my limited individual awareness related to the All-Encompassing consciousness of Neberdjer?

My response:

_____

_____

_____

Question 3: What obstacles prevent me from maintaining this awareness throughout daily activities?

My response:

_____

_____

_____

Question 4: How would my experience transform if I truly recognized all Creation as occurring within Neberdjer?

My response:

_____

_____

Question 5: What is the relationship between this contemplative awareness and the formal meditation practice to come?

My response:

_____

_____

_____

Visual Summary: The Three Levels of Mind

Draw or create a visual representation of how the wisdom you learned in this module relates in your own experience. Use any or all of the following: colors, symbols, hieroglyphs, codes, shapes, etc. in the open space below.

Module Completion Reflection

Before moving to the next module, assess your readiness:

Signs of Readiness:

☐ I understand Neberdjer as All-Encompassing Divinity underlying all Creation

☐ I can maintain awareness of Neberdjer with deliberate effort during contemplation

☐ I've attempted to maintain this awareness during daily activities

☐ I recognize this practice as preparation for formal Sau-Neberdjer meditation

☐ My contemplation practice demonstrates capacity for sustained awareness

☐ I've practiced consistently with this module and feel ready for meditation practice

Important: Remain with this module until these understandings stabilize.

Date completed: _____

What was the most significant insight you learned in this module:

_____
_____
_____
_____

MODULE 9: THE PRACTICE OF SAU-NEBERDJER CONSCIOUSNESS MEDITATION

TRANSITION MODULE: From Contemplation to Formal Meditation

Commentary on Amenemopet Chapter 9

Life Vitality Health

Understanding This Transition

Critical Recognition: Module 9 marks the pivotal transition from contemplative practice (Modules 1-8) to formal meditation. The section title changes here from 'Daily Contemplation Practice' to 'Daily Meditation Practice' and will remain so through Module 26.

In Modules 1-8, you practiced

Holding the meaning of focus phrases—staying with take-away teachings without continued analysis. This built your capacity for sustained attention and prepared your mind for the deeper work of formal meditation.

Now you begin

Sau-Neberdjer—the direct practice of recognizing consciousness itself as distinct from all mental and sensory content. This represents the essential shift from thinking about spiritual truths to directly recognizing the awareness observing those thoughts.

Quick Chapter Overview

Key Teaching: Sau-Neberdjer meditation cultivates recognition of your deeper self (Neberdjer) as source of the Soul-Aware-Witness-Self—the awareness that observes all mental and sensory phenomena without being identical to them. Therefore, in this practice discovering the Soul-Aware-Witness-Self leads to realization of Ab Neter (divine soul of every individual that sustains the Soul-Aware-Witness-Self) and recognition of Ab Neter's source as Neberdjer (All-Encompassing Divinity).

Main Principles:

- Sau-Neberdjer differs from contemplation—it recognizes awareness itself, not concepts about awareness
- Two starting practices: Visual (Apple Recognition) and Auditory (Sound Recognition)
- The practices help reveal that there is an 'I am' awareness—Soul-Aware-Witness-Self experiencing its own existence above the ordinary ego-level awareness
- Objects (apple, sound, thoughts, body) are used to experience how they appear WITHIN awareness; awareness is not the objects
- Throughout all changing phenomena, awareness remains constant and unchanging
- This practice transcends ego-mind to recognize awareness/consciousness itself as entity that is above the ego mind, senses and perceptions
- Sau-Neberdjer aims at metaphysical awakening, not merely psychological improvement or awareness of ordinary ego level perceptions and sensations.

Daily Meditation Practice

From this module forward, the practice section is titled 'Daily Meditation Practice' (not 'Daily Contemplation Practice'). Duration increases to 20-30 minutes.

TWO EXERCISES TO BEGIN THE PRACTICE OF INTROSPECTION

The Ancient Egyptian Book of Enlightenment Chapter 26 presents wisdom about a state of inner self-discovery by recognizing Soul-Aware-Witness-Self. From there awareness expands to discover the soul level of self (Ab-Neter) and from there the universal being (Neberdjer). The following exercises can be used to engage the process of introspection towards Soul-Aware-Witness-Self. Practice the pathway that resonates most naturally with you, or alternate between them. You may practice either.

PATHWAY 1: Visual Recognition Practice (The Apple)
Core Instruction:

With eyes open, sit comfortably and bring to mind an object—perhaps an apple resting on a table before you. You can use an actual apple or visualize one clearly. Notice how your eyes perceive its form: the roundness of its shape, the redness (or green) of its color, perhaps a stem extending from the top. Observe these visual qualities.

Now recognize:

'There is awareness of this apple.'

The apple exists as an object appearing within awareness. Your awareness knows the apple—but are you the apple? Obviously not. The apple is an object of perception, something appearing TO awareness. You remain as the awareness observing the apple.

Notice: Even if the apple disappears from view, awareness remains. Awareness existed before you looked at the apple, continues while observing the apple, and persists after attention moves elsewhere. The apple is temporary; awareness is constant.

The Essential Recognition:

This practice reveals a profound truth: You are not the objects you perceive—not the apple, not the thoughts about the apple, not even the body doing the perceiving. You are the awareness within which all these phenomena appear. This awareness—this 'I am' that knows—represents your essential nature as Soul-Aware-Witness-Self.

PATHWAY 2: Auditory Recognition Practice (Sound)

Core Instruction:

Sit quietly and notice sounds arising in your environment: perhaps traffic outside your window, a clock ticking in the room, birds singing in trees, or the subtle sound of your own breathing. With each sound that arises, recognize:

'There is awareness of this sound.'

The sound appears within awareness, exists briefly, then fades. Throughout—before the sound arose, while it existed, after it faded—awareness remained constant. The sounds come and go; awareness continues unchanging.

Notice: You are not identical to the sounds. Traffic sounds appear TO awareness; clock ticking appears TO awareness; breathing sounds appear TO awareness. But you—as awareness itself—remain distinct from all sounds that arise. The sounds are objects; you are the awareness observing those objects.

The Essential Recognition:

Like the visual pathway, this auditory practice reveals your nature as Soul-Aware-Witness-Self—the unchanging awareness within which all changing phenomena (sounds, thoughts, sensations) appear and disappear. You are the 'I am' that knows, not the temporary objects known.

COMPLETE PRACTICE INSTRUCTIONS (20-30 minutes)

Preparation

1. Choose your pathway (visual or auditory) for this session

2. Sit comfortably with spine naturally erect

3. Close eyes (for auditory pathway) or maintain soft gaze on object (for visual pathway)

4. Take three deep breaths to settle into presence

5. Set intention: 'I practice to recognize my essential nature as awareness itself'

Main Practice (15-25 minutes)

For Visual Pathway:

- Direct attention to chosen object (apple or other simple form)
- Observe its visual qualities without analysis
- Recognize: 'There is awareness of this object'
- Notice: Awareness knows the object; awareness is not the object
- Rest in recognition of yourself as the awareness observing
- When mind wanders into thoughts, gently return to recognition
- Continue alternating between observing object and recognizing awareness

For Auditory Pathway:

- Listen openly to sounds arising in environment
- With each sound, recognize: 'There is awareness of this sound'
- Notice: Awareness remains constant; sounds come and go
- Rest in recognition of yourself as the unchanging awareness
- When lost in thoughts, return to listening and recognizing awareness
- Continue recognizing: 'I am the awareness within which sounds appear'

Conclusion (3-5 minutes)

1. Gradually widen awareness to include body sensations

2. Recognize: 'Body sensations also appear within awareness'

3. Notice: Even this body is an object appearing TO awareness

4. Rest in simple recognition: 'I am the awareness observing all phenomena'

5. Take three deep breaths

6. Express gratitude for this recognition practice

7. Slowly open eyes (if closed) and return to activity

Working With Challenges

Challenge 1: 'I don't understand what awareness is'

Response: Don't try to understand awareness conceptually. Simply notice that right now, you are aware. Whatever is reading these words, whatever is aware of the room around you—THAT is awareness. You can't perceive awareness as an object (because it's the subject doing the perceiving), but you can recognize its presence directly.

Challenge 2: 'My mind keeps wandering into thoughts'

Response: Mind wandering is completely normal. When you notice wandering has occurred, recognize: 'There is awareness of these thoughts.' The thoughts are objects appearing within awareness. You—as awareness—remained present even while thoughts arose. Simply return to recognizing awareness observing.

Challenge 3: 'This feels too abstract or intellectual'

Response: This practice IS direct—more direct than contemplating concepts. You're not thinking about awareness; you're recognizing the awareness that's already present, already observing. Stay with the simple recognition: 'I am aware.' That 'I am'—that's what you're recognizing.

Practice Log

Session 1

Date: _____ Duration: _____ Pathway Used: _____

Key recognitions or challenges:

_____

_____

Session 2

Date: _____ Duration: _____ Pathway Used: _____

Key recognitions or challenges:

_____

_____

Session 3

Date: _____ Duration: _____ Pathway Used: _____

Key recognitions or challenges:

_____

_____

Session 4

Date: _____ Duration: _____ Pathway Used: _____

Key recognitions or challenges:

_____

_____

Visual Summary: The Three Levels of Mind

Draw or create a visual representation of how the wisdom you learned in this module relates in your own experience. Use any or all of the following: colors, symbols, hieroglyphs, codes, shapes, etc. in the open space below.

Module Completion Reflection

Module 9 establishes the foundation for all subsequent meditation stages. Spend sufficient time here to establish basic recognition of Soul-Aware-Witness-Self.

Signs of Readiness to Progress:

☐ I can sustain 20-30 minutes of recognition practice

☐ I've experienced moments of recognizing awareness distinct from mental content

☐ I understand the difference between contemplating concepts and recognizing awareness

☐ Both pathways feel accessible (even if one feels more natural)

☐ I can gently return to recognition when mind wanders

☐ I feel ready to deepen this recognition through progressive stages

Important: Module 9 establishes the foundation for Modules 10-15 (progressive meditation stages) and Modules 16-26 (Gentle Return integration). Take your time here. There is no benefit in rushing forward without establishing this basic recognition.

Date completed: _____

What was the most significant insight you learned in this module from this module:

_____
_____
_____
_____

MODULE 10: Divine Providence Versus Worldly Scheming

Difficulty Level: ● Advanced

Commentary on Amenemopet Chapter 6B VIII-IX

Daily Reflection Practice

Choose a verse from the Chapter 6B VIII-IX to work with each day.

Read Dr. Ashby's translation and commentary carefully. Then write your reflections about what this teaching means in your life today. How does it expose aryu patterns? What resistance arises? Where do you see this teaching reflected in your daily experiences?

Reflection 1

Date: _____ Verse: _____

My reflections:

_____

_____

_____

Reflection 2

Date: _____ Verse: _____

My reflections:

_____

_____

_____

Reflection 3

Date: _____ Verse: _____

My reflections:

_____

_____

_____

Reflection 4

Date: _____ Verse: _____

My reflections:

_____

_____

_____

Reflection 5

Date: _____ Verse: _____

My reflections:

_____

_____

_____

Daily Contemplation Practice (15-20 minutes)

After your written reflection, sit in contemplation with a focus phrase from this module's teachings. Having practiced reflection, now sit while holding the meaning of the focus phrase. Holding is not continuing to reflect or think about it. Rather it means staying with the take-away meaning of the teaching for an extended period. You have already reflected; now stay with the meaning as you understand it currently. If the mind wanders, simply bring it back to the take-away objective of the focus phrase.

Focus Phrases for Contemplation

Choose one phrase to hold in contemplation:

- "I accept the measure given by the Divine through providence"
- "Life circumstances reflect accumulated aryu and divine providence"
- "Weakness of mind generates cunning and unrighteous schemes"
- "Poverty in the hand of the Divine is glorifying and beneficial"
- "Material power with shennu (anguish, strife, anxiety) is spiritual poverty"
- "Sweetness in hat (conscious awareness) with simple provisions aligned with Divine"

Contemplation Practice Log

Session 1

Date: _____ Focus phrase used: _____

Insights from staying with this meaning:

_____

Session 2

Date: _____ Focus phrase used: _____

Insights from staying with this meaning:

_____

_____

Session 3

Date: _____ Focus phrase used: _____

Insights from staying with this meaning:

_____

_____

Session 4

Date: _____ Focus phrase used: _____

Insights from staying with this meaning:

_____

_____

Daily Meditation Practice (20-30 minutes)

Stage I: Focused Attention with Name and Form

Using Visual Representation and Audible Hekau Repetition

STAGE OVERVIEW

This foundational stage develops capacity for sustained attention by combining visual focus (deity image or symbol) with audible repetition of sacred sounds (hekau/mantras). The practice establishes concentrated awareness on an external object representing divine consciousness, training the mind to maintain steady attention while aryu patterns attempting to pull awareness into habitual thought streams.

PRACTICE INSTRUCTIONS

- Sit comfortably facing an image or symbol of divine form (Asar/Aset/Ra/Maat)
- Begin with three deep breaths to settle body and mind
- Gaze softly at the image without straining eyes
- Begin audible repetition of the deity's hekau (e.g., 'Om Asar Aset Heru' or chosen sacred name)
- Coordinate breath with repetition naturally
- When mind wanders, gently return attention to visual form and audible sound
- Allow meaning of divine name to resonate without intellectual analysis
- Maintain practice for 20-30 minutes with gentle persistence

PROFICIENCY INDICATORS

Ready to progress to Stage II when:

☐ Can maintain sustained attention on form and sound for 15-20 minutes with minimal wandering

☐ Mind returns to practice more quickly when distraction occurs

☐ Experience deepening connection with divine form beyond intellectual concept

☐ Begin recognizing awareness itself that observes both form and sound

Practice Log

Session 1

Date: _____ Duration: _____

Observations:

_____

_____

Session 2

Date: _____ Duration: _____

Observations:

_____

_____

Session 3

Date: _____ Duration: _____

Observations:

_____

_____

Session 4

Date: _____ Duration: _____

Observations:

_____

_____

Session 5

Date: _____ Duration: _____

Observations:

_____

_____

Session 6

Date: _____ Duration: _____

Observations:

_____

_____

Reference: For complete teachings on this stage, see Chapter 9 of the main book.

Visual Summary: The Three Levels of Mind

Draw or create a visual representation of how the wisdom you learned in this module relates in your own experience. Use any or all of the following: colors, symbols, hieroglyphs, codes, shapes, etc. in the open space below.

MODULE 11: Power-Seeking, Mental Wandering, and Divine Providence

Meditation Stage II: Subtle Focused Attention with Mental Visualization

Daily Reflection Practice

Choose a verse from the Amenemopet Chapter 7, Verses 10-15 to work with each day.

Read Dr. Ashby's translation and commentary carefully. Then write your reflections about what this teaching means in your life today. How does it expose aryu patterns? What resistance arises? Where do you see this teaching reflected in your daily experiences?

Reflection 1

Date: _____ Verse: _____

My reflections:

_____

_____

_____

Reflection 2

Date: _____ Verse: _____

My reflections:

_____

_____

_____

Reflection 3

Date: _____ Verse: _____

My reflections:

_____

_____

_____

Reflection 4

Date: _____ Verse: _____

My reflections:

_____

_____

_____

Daily Contemplation Practice (15-20 minutes)

After your written reflection, sit in contemplation with a focus phrase from this module's teachings. Having practiced reflection, now sit while holding the meaning of the focus phrase. Holding is not continuing to reflect or think about it. Rather it means staying with the take-away meaning of the teaching for an extended period. You have already reflected; now stay with the meaning as you understand it currently. If the mind wanders, simply bring it back to the take-away objective of the focus phrase.

Focus Phrases for Contemplation

Based on Commentary on Amenemopet Chapter 7, Verses 10-15

Choose one phrase to hold in contemplation:

- "I refrain from creating schemes through deliberate volition"
- "Mental wandering in pursuit of domination generates wrong action"
- "Every person belongs to their time; providence operates through aryu"
- "Trusting divine providence frees mind from heated manipulation"
- "Silent trust in divine timing conserves vital energy for spiritual growth"

Contemplation Practice Log

Session 1

Date: _____ Focus phrase used: _____

Insights:

_____

_____

Session 2

Date: _____ Focus phrase used: _____

Insights:

_____

_____

Session 3

Date: _____ Focus phrase used: _____

Insights:

_____

_____

Session 4

Date: _____ Focus phrase used: _____

Insights:

_____

_____

Daily Meditation Practice (20-30 minutes)

Continue building on Module 10's foundation with this progressive stage.

Stage Overview

Stage II internalizes practice. Release external visual object and audible chanting. Instead, mentally visualize the hieroglyphs or deity form while internally repeating the hekau. This develops capacity for sustained attention on internally generated objects—more subtle than external anchors and requiring refined concentration.

Practice Instructions

- Sit with eyes closed
- Mentally visualize the divine symbol or hieroglyphic form clearly
- Internally repeat the hekau (divine name) in rhythm with visualization
- Hold both mental image and internal sound simultaneously
- When visualization fades or mind wanders, gently refresh the image
- Continue for 10-20 minutes
- End by releasing the visualization and resting in open awareness

Proficiency Indicators

You're ready to progress when:

☐ Maintain clear mental visualization for 10-20 minutes

☐ Internal repetition flows naturally without forced effort

☐ Experience stable focus on internally generated objects

☐ Feel ready to release form and work with qualities (moving toward Stage III)

Practice Log

Session 1

Date: _____ Duration: _____

Key experiences:

_____

_____

Session 2

Date: _____ Duration: _____

Key experiences:

_____

_____

Session 3

Date: _____ Duration: _____

Key experiences:

_____

_____

Session 4

Date: _____ Duration: _____

Key experiences:

_____

_____

Session 5

Date: _____ Duration: _____

Key experiences:

_____

_____

Note: For complete stage instructions and detailed guidance, see Chapter 9 of the main book. These modules provide practice framework; the book provides comprehensive teaching.

Visual Summary: The Three Levels of Mind

Draw or create a visual representation of how the wisdom you learned in this module relates in your own experience. Use any or all of the following: colors, symbols, hieroglyphs, codes, shapes, etc. in the open space below.

MODULE 12: Transforming Destiny Through Purification

Difficulty Level: Intermediate

Meditation Stage III: Open Monitoring with Neberdjer Qualities

Daily Reflection Practice

Choose a verse from the Amenemopet Chapter 7 to work with each day.

Read Dr. Ashby's translation and commentary carefully. Then write your reflections about what this teaching means in your life today. How does it expose aryu patterns? What resistance arises? Where do you see this teaching reflected in your daily experiences?

Reflection 1

Date: _____ Verse: _____

My reflections:

_____

_____

_____

Reflection 2

Date: _____ Verse: _____

My reflections:

_____

_____

_____

Reflection 3

Date: _____ Verse: _____

My reflections:

_____

_____

_____

Daily Contemplation Practice (15-20 minutes)

After your written reflection, sit in contemplation with a focus phrase from this module's teachings. Having practiced reflection, now sit while holding the meaning of the focus phrase. Holding is not continuing to reflect or think about it. Rather it means staying with the take-away meaning of the teaching for an extended period. You have already reflected; now stay with the meaning as you understand it currently. If the mind wanders, simply bring it back to the take-away objective of the focus phrase.

Focus Phrases for Contemplation

Based on Addendum to Commentary on Chapter 12 in Dr. Ashby's book is titled "Addendum to Chapter 11 about Amenemopet Chapter 7: Transforming Destiny Through Purification"

Choose one phrase to hold in contemplation:

- "My destiny transforms as aryu patterns thin through practice"
- "Purification of ab (unconscious) reveals Ab-Neter awareness"
- "Each righteous choice creates new aryu supporting transformation"
- "Divine providence operates through accumulated spiritual merit"

Contemplation Practice Log

Session 1

Date: _____ Focus phrase used: _____

Insights:

_____

Session 2

Date: _____ Focus phrase used: _____

Insights:

_____

Session 3

Date: _____ Focus phrase used: _____

Insights:

_____

Session 4

Date: _____ Focus phrase used: _____

Insights:

_____

Daily Meditation Practice (20-30 minutes)
Continue building on Module 11's foundation with this progressive stage.

Stage Overview

Stage III represents fundamental shift from focused attention to open awareness. Release all auditory expression, mental repetition, and visual objects. Instead, maintain wide-open awareness while holding Neberdjer's qualities as conceptual framework: All-Encompassing, All-Pervading, Infinite, Eternal. Recognize all phenomena as expressions of these divine qualities.

Practice Instructions

- Sit with eyes closed, releasing all visual and auditory anchors
- Maintain open, receptive awareness without focusing on any particular object
- Hold Neberdjer epithets as background framework: 'All-Encompassing Existence,' 'Consciousness Underlying All'
- When sound arises, recognize: 'Neberdjer hearing through this form'
- When thought appears, note: 'Neberdjer thinking through this mind'
- When sensation emerges, acknowledge: 'Neberdjer experiencing through this body'
- Allow all phenomena to arise and pass without engagement or suppression
- Continue for 10-20 minutes

Proficiency Indicators

You're ready to progress when:

☐ Rest in open awareness for 10-20 minutes maintaining Neberdjer framework

☐ Thoughts arise without capturing attention into storylines

☐ Experience equanimity toward all arising phenomena

☐ Feel ready to work with paradox (moving toward Stage IV)

Practice Log

Session 1

Date: _____ Duration: _____

Key experiences:

_____

Session 2

Date: _____ Duration: _____

Key experiences:

_____

Session 3

Date: _____ Duration: _____

Key experiences:

_____

Session 4

Date: _____ Duration: _____

Key experiences:

_____

Note: For complete stage instructions and detailed guidance, see Chapter 9 of the main book. These modules provide practice framework; the book provides comprehensive teaching.

Visual Summary: The Three Levels of Mind

Draw or create a visual representation of how the wisdom you learned in this module relates in your own experience. Use any or all of the following: colors, symbols, hieroglyphs, codes, shapes, etc. in the open space below.

MODULE 13: Commentary on Chapter 7B

Meditation Stage IV: Hermetic Wisdom-Meditation - Dissolving Dualities

Daily Reflection Practice

Choose a verse from the Amenemopet Chapter 7B, Verses 10-12 to work with each day.

Read Dr. Ashby's translation and commentary carefully. Then write your reflections about what this teaching means in your life today. How does it expose aryu patterns? What resistance arises? Where do you see this teaching reflected in your daily experiences?

Reflection 1

Date: _____ Verse: _____

My reflections:

_____

_____

_____

Reflection 2

Date: _____ Verse: _____

My reflections:

_____

_____

_____

Reflection 3

Date: _____ Verse: _____

My reflections:

_____

_____

_____

Reflection 4

Date: _____ Verse: _____

My reflections:

_____

_____

_____

Daily Contemplation Practice (15-20 minutes)

After your written reflection, sit in contemplation with a focus phrase from this module's teachings. Having practiced reflection, now sit while holding the meaning of the focus phrase. Holding is not continuing to reflect or think about it. Rather it means staying with the take-away meaning of the teaching for an extended period. You have already reflected; now stay with the meaning as you understand it currently. If the mind wanders, simply bring it back to the take-away objective of the focus phrase.

Focus Phrases for Contemplation

Based on Commentary on Amenemopet Chapter 7B, Verses 10-12

Choose one phrase to hold in contemplation:

- "I observe how aryu patterns drive heated reactions"
- "Silent mind emerges as aryu patterns thin through practice"
- "Recognition of reactive patterns represents first step toward freedom"
- "Patience with transformation process honors natural purification timing"

Contemplation Practice Log

Session 1

Date: _____ Focus phrase used: _____

Insights:

_____

Session 2

Date: _____ Focus phrase used: _____

Insights:

_____

Session 3

Date: _____ Focus phrase used: _____

Insights:

_____

Session 4

Date: _____ Focus phrase used: _____

Insights:

_____

Daily Meditation Practice (20-30 minutes)

Continue building on Module 12's foundation with this progressive stage.

Stage Overview

Stage IV uses Hermetic contemplations to exhaust dualistic thinking. Work with paradoxical truths: 'Neberdjer is beyond space, yet Neberdjer is all space.' Hold both aspects simultaneously until dualistic mind reaches its limit and falls silent. This reveals the non-dual awareness underlying all mental activity.

Practice Instructions

- Begin with Stage III open awareness
- Phase 1: Contemplate first pole of paradox (10 minutes) - e.g., 'Neberdjer transcends all forms'
- Phase 2: Contemplate opposite pole (10 minutes) - e.g., 'Neberdjer IS all forms'
- Phase 3: Hold BOTH simultaneously - let mind struggle with the contradiction
- Continue holding the paradox without trying to resolve it mentally
- Watch as dualistic thinking exhausts itself
- Rest in the silence that emerges when concepts dissolve
- Practice 1-2 times weekly, supplementing basic Stage III practice

Proficiency Indicators

You're ready to progress when:

☐ Each contemplation naturally concludes in pause where dualistic thinking ceases

☐ Phase 3 silence sustains for 5+ minutes with minimal thought intrusion

☐ Experience glimpses of non-dual awareness beyond subject-object split

☐ Feel ready to drop conceptual framework entirely (moving toward Stage V)

Practice Log

Session 1

Date: _____ Duration: _____

Key experiences:

_____

Session 2

Date: _____ Duration: _____

Key experiences:

_____

Session 3

Date: _____ Duration: _____

Key experiences:

_____

Session 4

Date: _____ Duration: _____

Key experiences:

_____

Session 5

Date: _____ Duration: _____

Key experiences:

_____

Note: For complete stage instructions and detailed guidance, see Chapter 9 of the main book. These modules provide practice framework; the book provides comprehensive teaching.

Visual Summary: The Three Levels of Mind

Draw or create a visual representation of how the wisdom you learned in this module relates in your own experience. Use any or all of the following: colors, symbols, hieroglyphs, codes, shapes, etc. in the open space below.

MODULE 14: The Serpent Power of Righteousness

Meditation Stage V: Open Monitoring with Abstract Awareness

Daily Reflection Practice

Choose a verse from the Chapter 8, Verses 19-20 to work with each day.

Read Dr. Ashby's translation and commentary carefully. Then write your reflections about what this teaching means in your life today. How does it expose aryu patterns? What resistance arises? Where do you see this teaching reflected in your daily experiences?

Reflection 1

Date: _____ Verse: _____

My reflections:

_____

_____

_____

Reflection 2

Date: _____ Verse: _____

My reflections:

_____

_____

_____

Reflection 3

Date: _____ Verse: _____

My reflections:

_____

_____

_____

Reflection 4

Date: _____ Verse: _____

My reflections:

_____

_____

_____

Daily Contemplation Practice (15-20 minutes)

After your written reflection, sit in contemplation with a focus phrase from this module's teachings. Having practiced reflection, now sit while holding the meaning of the focus phrase. Holding is not continuing to reflect or think about it. Rather it means staying with the take-away meaning of the teaching for an extended period. You have already reflected; now stay with the meaning as you understand it currently. If the mind wanders, simply bring it back to the take-away objective of the focus phrase.

Focus Phrases for Contemplation

Based on Commentary on Amenemopet Chapter 8, Verses 19-20

Choose one phrase to hold in contemplation:

- "Righteousness (Maat) operates as serpent power protecting consciousness"
- "Ethical living generates protective force field around personality"
- "Serpent power of Maat repels destructive influences automatically"

Contemplation Practice Log

Session 1

Date: _____ Focus phrase used: _____

Insights:

_____

Session 2

Date: _____ Focus phrase used: _____

Insights:

_____

Session 3

Date: _____ Focus phrase used: _____

Insights:

_____

Session 4

Date: _____ Focus phrase used: _____

Insights:

_____

Session 5

Date: _____ Focus phrase used: _____

Insights:

_____

Daily Meditation Practice (20-30 minutes)

Continue building on Module 13's foundation with this progressive stage.

Stage Overview

Stage V releases even Neberdjer epithets and conceptual descriptions. Rest in pure witness consciousness—awareness observing mental and sensory contents without identifying with them. The sense of individual observer remains ('I am aware') but with minimal mental commentary. This embodies Soul-Aware-Witness-Self recognition.

Practice Instructions

- Sit with eyes closed, releasing all conceptual frameworks
- Maintain awareness itself without conceptual support
- Simply observe: sounds arise and pass, thoughts emerge and dissolve, sensations appear and disappear
- Rest as the witness—the awareness observing all phenomena
- Notice: clear sense of observer distinct from observed content
- Allow minimal mental interference or commentary
- Continue for 15-30 minutes

Proficiency Indicators

You're ready to progress when:

☐ Sustain witness consciousness for 15-30 minutes

☐ Experience clear sense of observer distinct from observed

☐ Minimal mental commentary arises during practice

☐ Recognize consciousness as distinct from thoughts, emotions, sensations it observes

☐ Feel ready to question even the witnessing (moving toward Stage VI)

Practice Log
Session 1

Date: _____ Duration: _____

Key experiences:

_____

Session 2

Date: _____ Duration: _____

Key experiences:

_____

Session 3

Date: _____ Duration: _____

Key experiences:

_____

Session 4

Date: _____ Duration: _____

Key experiences:

_____

Session 5

Date: _____ Duration: _____

Key experiences:

_____

Note: For complete stage instructions and detailed guidance, see Chapter 9 of the main book. These modules provide practice framework; the book provides comprehensive teaching.

Visual Summary: The Three Levels of Mind

Draw or create a visual representation of how the wisdom you learned in this module relates in your own experience. Use any or all of the following: colors, symbols, hieroglyphs, codes, shapes, etc. in the open space below.

MODULE 15: Speech, Vitality, and the Path to Inner Sanctuary

Meditation Stage VI: Non-Dual Awareness - Individuation Falling Away

Daily Reflection Practice

Choose a verse from the Amenemopet Chapter 8X and 8XI to work with each day.

Read Dr. Ashby's translation and commentary carefully. Then write your reflections about what this teaching means in your life today. How does it expose aryu patterns? What resistance arises? Where do you see this teaching reflected in your daily experiences?

Reflection 1

Date: _____ Verse: _____

My reflections:

_____

_____

_____

Reflection 2

Date: _____ Verse: _____

My reflections:

_____

_____

_____

Reflection 3

Date: _____ Verse: _____

My reflections:

_____

_____

_____

Reflection 4

Date: _____ Verse: _____

My reflections:

_____

_____

_____

Daily Contemplation Practice (15-20 minutes)

After your written reflection, sit in contemplation with a focus phrase from this module's teachings. Having practiced reflection, now sit while holding the meaning of the focus phrase. Holding is not continuing to reflect or think about it. Rather it means staying with the take-away meaning of the teaching for an extended period. You have already reflected; now stay with the meaning as you understand it currently. If the mind wanders, simply bring it back to the take-away objective of the focus phrase.

Focus Phrases for Contemplation

Based on Commentary on Amenemopet Chapter 8X and 8XI

Choose one phrase to hold in contemplation:

- "Speech quality reveals ab (unconscious mind) condition"
- "Path to kara (inner sanctuary) requires purified communication"
- "Silent speech practice thins aryu preventing Ab-Neter recognition"

Contemplation Practice Log

Session 1

Date: _____ Focus phrase used: _____

Insights:

_____

Session 2

Date: _____ Focus phrase used: _____

Insights:

_____

Session 3

Date: _____ Focus phrase used: _____

Insights:

_____

Daily Meditation Practice (20-30 minutes)

Continue building on Module 14's foundation with this progressive stage.

Stage Overview

Stage VI represents the culmination: even the sense of individual witness dissolves. Rather than 'I am aware of phenomena,' recognition becomes 'awareness is.' No separate observer remains—only awareness aware of itself. This is Ab-Neter recognition: consciousness recognizing its own divine nature as Neberdjer expressing through apparent individuation.

Practice Instructions

- Begin with Stage V witness consciousness
- Turn attention toward the witness itself: 'What is this awareness that observes?'
- Notice: awareness cannot be objectified (it's the subject observing)
- Recognize: awareness is not limited to this body-mind
- Allow the boundary between 'me' (individual) and 'awareness' (universal) to dissolve
- Rest as awareness aware of itself—no separate observer
- This is Ab-Neter recognition: divine consciousness recognizing its own nature
- Continue for 20-30 minutes

Proficiency Indicators

You're ready to progress when:

☐ Experience periods where sense of separate observer dissolves

☐ Recognition arises: 'awareness is' (not 'I am aware')

☐ Feel direct recognition of Ab-Neter as your essential nature

☐ Glimpses of awareness recognizing itself as Neberdjer

☐ Ready to stabilize this recognition through Gentle Return practice (Modules 16-26)

Practice Log

Session 1

Date: _____ Duration: _____

Key experiences:

_____

Session 2

Date: _____ Duration: _____

Key experiences:

_____

Session 3

Date: _____ Duration: _____

Key experiences:

_____

Session 4

Date: _____ Duration: _____

Key experiences:

_____

Note: For complete stage instructions and detailed guidance, see Chapter 9 of the main book. These modules provide practice framework; the book provides comprehensive teaching.

Visual Summary: The Three Levels of Mind

Draw or create a visual representation of how the wisdom you learned in this module relates in your own experience. Use any or all of the following: colors, symbols, hieroglyphs, codes, shapes, etc. in the open space below.

MODULE 16: Avoiding Heated Persons - Self-Control and Compassion

Difficulty Level: ● Advanced - FOUNDATION MODULE

Commentary on Amenemopet Chapter 9XI-9XII

Understanding Your Journey to This Point

You have now completed Modules 1-15, establishing a comprehensive foundation for consciousness transformation. Let's recognize what you've accomplished:

- Modules 1-8: You practiced contemplation, learning to hold teaching meanings without continued analysis, building your capacity for sustained attention while the philosophy of wisdom absorption penetrated from hat (conscious mind) to ab (unconscious mind).
- Module 9: You transitioned to formal Sau-Neberdjer meditation, beginning to recognize yourself as Soul-Aware-Witness-Self—the awareness observing all phenomena rather than being identical to thoughts, sensations, and perceptions.
- Modules 10-15: You progressed through six meditation stages, developing from focused attention on external objects to recognition of non-dual awareness where even the sense of individual witness dissolves into pure consciousness recognizing its own divine nature.

Through these fifteen modules, you've developed significant capacity:

- The ability to sustain meditation practice for 20-30 minutes

- Recognition of awareness as distinct from mental content

- Experience of witness consciousness observing phenomena

- Glimpses of Ab-Neter awareness—consciousness recognizing its divine foundation

- Understanding of the progressive stages from form to formless meditation

The Challenge You Now Face:

Despite these accomplishments, you've likely noticed a persistent challenge: during formal meditation practice, you experience periods of recognition—sometimes profound, sometimes subtle—but when you return to daily activities, that recognition often disappears. The mind that rested as witness consciousness during practice becomes identified with thoughts, reactions, and habitual patterns during work, relationships, and routine activities.

This gap between formal practice and daily life represents the crucial challenge that Modules 16-26 address through what the teaching calls 'Gentle Return Practice.'

Daily Reflection Practice

Choose a verse from the Amenemopet Chapter 9XI-9XII to work with each day.

Read Dr. Ashby's translation and commentary carefully. Then write your reflections about what this teaching means in your life today. How does it expose aryu patterns? What resistance arises? Where do you see this teaching reflected in your daily experiences?

Reflection 1

Date: _____ Verse: _____

My reflections:

_____

_____

_____

Reflection 2

Date: _____ Verse: _____

My reflections:

_____

_____

_____

Reflection 3

Date: _____ Verse: _____

My reflections:

_____

_____

_____

THE GENTLE RETURN: Working with Mind Wandering During Practice

A crucial understanding must be established regarding the natural tendency of mind to wander during these recognition practices.

Consider what occurs: You follow the visual or auditory pathway and discover the 'I am'—the Soul-Aware-Witness-Self experiencing its own existence independent of objects. Yet after a period, you suddenly realize that awareness has become absorbed in thoughts—planning, remembering, analyzing, or simply drifting through mental imagery.

What has occurred? The 'I am' awareness has become 'identified' with thoughts arising in consciousness. Instead of remaining as witness observing mental phenomena, awareness has reverted to the habitual pattern of experiencing itself as identical with those thoughts. During this period of identification, the Soul-Aware-Witness-Self 'forgets itself,' absorbed in mental content.

This forgetting represents not a new occurrence but rather the default pattern operating throughout most of life—the habit of un-mindfulness about the 'I am' as oneself, reinforced through countless repetitions across years and, according to the teaching, lifetimes.

The Practice of Gentle Return

The wisdom to be understood: the crucial moment in practice occurs not when recognition remains stable but when you notice that wandering has occurred. This noticing—'Oh, I have been absorbed in thoughts'—itself represents Soul-Aware-Witness-Self awareness emerging. When this recognition arises, practice gentle return:

Do not judge the wandering: Resist criticizing yourself for losing awareness or generating frustration. Such judgment perpetuates identification with thinking rather than supporting recognition of the witness. The wandering occurred because accumulated aryu patterns create strong habitual pull toward thought-identification—this represents mechanical conditioning, not personal failing.

Do not attempt forceful control: Avoid straining to maintain Soul-Aware-Witness-Self recognition through willful effort. Such forcing creates tension that itself becomes an object occupying awareness. The practice seeks revelation of what already exists, not creation of a special state through mental effort.

Simply return awareness gently: When noticing that wandering has occurred, allow awareness to gently disengage from thought content and return to recognition of itself as witness. This return possesses a quality of softness, ease, and acceptance—like a mother softly redirecting a wandering child with patience and kindness rather than harsh discipline.

Gradual Stabilization Through Patient Repetition

Through repeated gentle returns—perhaps dozens of times within a single practice session—consciousness gradually stabilizes:

- The gap between wandering and recognition shortens. Initially, minutes may pass before noticing absorption in thoughts. With repetition, you notice wandering beginning to occur rather than only recognizing it after prolonged absorption.
- Stability gradually increases. Soul-Aware-Witness-Self recognition may initially sustain for only moments before reverting to thought-identification. Through patient practice, these moments extend to sustained periods where awareness remains as witness.
- Aryu patterns gradually thin. Each gentle return creates new aryu supporting witness-awareness rather than thought-identification. These accumulate gradually, competing with and eventually outweighing the dense aryu patterns of habitual un-mindfulness. The thinning occurs through patient accumulation of correct recognition repeated countless times.

The Teaching About Non-Striving

This gentle return practice does not aim to eliminate thoughts or to maintain constant Soul-Aware-Witness-Self recognition through forceful concentration. The practice simply involves recognizing awareness as witness when recognition naturally emerges and gently returning to that recognition when noticing that identification with mental content has occurred.

There is no failure in wandering, but there is achievement in recognition and return—the patient, compassionate process of allowing awareness to become familiar with its true nature through repeated exposure; and from there maturing to realize its essence as universal consciousness.

Consider the metaphor of sunlight penetrating morning mist: The sun does not force the mist to dissolve through violent effort. It simply continues shining, and the mist naturally dissipates through gradual warming. Similarly, each gentle return contributes to progressive thinning of accumulated patterns. Through countless gentle returns, repeated patiently across practice sessions, consciousness gradually stabilizes in self-recognition rather than remaining perpetually lost in identification with mental-emotional content.

Therefore, approach these practices with patience, gentleness, and trust in the process. The wandering will occur—this is certain. The gentle return represents your response, repeated as many times as necessary, with the understanding that each return contributes to the gradual stabilization that ultimately allows consciousness to rest in its own true nature.

Daily Contemplation Practice (15-20 minutes)

After your written reflection, sit in contemplation with a focus phrase from this module's teachings. Having practiced reflection, now sit while holding the meaning of the focus phrase. Holding is not continuing to reflect or think about it. Rather it means staying with the take-away meaning of the teaching for an extended period. You have already reflected; now stay with the meaning as you understand it currently. If the mind wanders, simply bring it back to the take-away objective of the focus phrase.

Focus Phrases for Contemplation

Choose one phrase to hold in contemplation (based on Amenemopet Chapter 9XI-9XII*):*

- "I recognize heated persons (shemm) by their agitated patterns"
- "Compassionate distance protects my purification practice"
- "Divine transformation requires choosing supportive spiritual environment"

Contemplation Practice Log

Session 1

Date: _____ Focus phrase used: _____

Insights:

_____

_____

Session 2

Date: _____ Focus phrase used: _____

Insights:

_____

_____

Session 3

Date: _____ Focus phrase used: _____

Insights:

_____

_____

Session 4

Date: _____ Focus phrase used: _____

Insights:

_____

_____

Session 5

Date: _____ Focus phrase used: _____

Insights:

_____

_____

Session 6

Date: _____ Focus phrase used: _____

Insights:

_____

_____

_____

Daily Meditation Practice (30-45 minutes)

Beginning with Module 16, practice duration increases to 30-45 minutes as you integrate Gentle Return practice.

LESSON 1: Breath Awareness with Gentle Return

INSIGHT: Why Begin with Breath

The breath serves as ideal anchor for developing Gentle Return practice because it remains constantly available, operates automatically without volition, and provides neutral object of attention that carries minimal emotional charge or conceptual complexity.

Unlike visual objects requiring eyes open or mental repetition requiring active generation, breath awareness functions whether eyes open or closed, whether sitting formally or moving through daily activities. This universality makes breath the perfect foundation for practices that will eventually extend beyond formal meditation into all moments of life.

PRACTICE: Breath Awareness with Gentle Return

1. Sit comfortably with spine naturally erect, hands resting in lap

2. Close eyes or maintain soft downward gaze

3. Take three deep, conscious breaths to settle into presence

4. Allow breath to return to natural rhythm without controlling it

5. Direct attention to the sensation of breathing—perhaps at nostrils where air enters and exits, or at abdomen rising and falling

6. Simply observe breath without changing it: 'There is awareness of breathing'

7. When you notice mind has wandered into thoughts, practice Gentle Return:

8. • Notice without judgment: 'Ah, I've been thinking'

9. • Recognize this noticing itself as awareness emerging

10. • Gently, kindly return attention to breath sensation

11. • No forcing, no frustration—just soft return

12. Continue for 30-45 minutes, returning gently each time wandering is noticed

13. Count your gentle returns if helpful—celebrate high numbers as they represent practice working

14. End by taking three deep breaths and expressing gratitude for practice

Proficiency Indicators

You're ready to progress to Lesson 2 when you can:

☐ Sustain 30-45 minutes of practice with breath as primary anchor

☐ Notice mind wandering within seconds or minutes rather than being lost for long periods

☐ Return gently without self-criticism most of the time

☐ Experience the return itself as recognition (awareness emerging) rather than failure

☐ Feel increasing familiarity with the quality of witness-awareness observing breath and thoughts

Practice Log

Session 1

Date: _____ Duration: _____

Approximate number of gentle returns: _____

Key insights:

_____

_____

Session 2

Date: _____ Duration: _____

Approximate number of gentle returns: _____

Key insights:

_____

_____

Session 3

Date: _____ Duration: _____

Approximate number of gentle returns: _____

Key insights:

_____

_____

Session 4

Date: _____ Duration: _____

Approximate number of gentle returns: _____

Key insights:

_____

_____

Session 5

Date: _____ Duration: _____

Approximate number of gentle returns: _____

Key insights:

_____

_____

Session 6

Date: _____ Duration: _____

Approximate number of gentle returns: _____

Key insights:

_____

_____

Session 7

Date: _____ Duration: _____

Approximate number of gentle returns: _____

Key insights:

_____

_____

Visual Summary: The Three Levels of Mind

Draw or create a visual representation of how the wisdom you learned in this module relates in your own experience. Use any or all of the following: colors, symbols, hieroglyphs, codes, shapes, etc. in the open space below.

MODULE 17: The Corruption of Greed and False Oaths

Difficulty Level: ● Advanced

Commentary on Amenemopet Chapter 11

Daily Reflection Practice

Choose a verse from the --------- to work with each day.

Read Dr. Ashby's translation and commentary carefully. Then write your reflections about what this teaching means in your life today. How does it expose aryu patterns? What resistance arises? Where do you see this teaching reflected in your daily experiences?

Reflection 1

Date: _____ Verse: _____

My reflections:

_____

_____

_____

Reflection 2

Date: _____ Verse: _____

My reflections:

_____

_____

_____

Reflection 3

Date: _____ Verse: _____

My reflections:

_____

_____

_____

Reflection 4

Date: _____ Verse: _____

My reflections:

_____

_____

_____

Daily Contemplation Practice (15-20 minutes)

After your written reflection, sit in contemplation with a focus phrase from this module's teachings. Having practiced reflection, now sit while holding the meaning of the focus phrase. Holding is not continuing to reflect or think about it. Rather it means staying with the take-away meaning of the teaching for an extended period. You have already reflected; now stay with the meaning as you understand it currently. If the mind wanders, simply bring it back to the take-away objective of the focus phrase.

Focus Phrases for Contemplation

Choose one phrase to hold in contemplation:

- "Greed operates as a dense aryu pattern obscuring Ab-Neter awareness"
- "Truth-speaking aligns personality with divine consciousness"
- "Corruption begins in mind before manifesting in action"

Contemplation Practice Log

Session 1

Date: _____ Focus phrase used: _____

Insights:

_____

_____

Session 2

Date: _____ Focus phrase used: _____

Insights:

_____

_____

Session 3

Date: _____ Focus phrase used: _____

Insights:

_____

_____

Session 4

Date: _____ Focus phrase used: _____

Insights:

_____

_____

Session 5

Date: _____ Focus phrase used: _____

Insights:

_____

_____

Daily Meditation Practice (30-45 minutes)

LESSON 2: Sound Awareness with Gentle Return

INSIGHT

Sound provides a different gateway for developing gentle return practice because auditory phenomena possess temporal qualities that visual objects lack. A sound arises, exists for a duration, and dissolves back into silence—revealing the impermanent nature of all experiences. Throughout the entire arc of a sound—the arising, presence, and dissolving—awareness remains constant and unchanging. This reveals a profound truth: awareness does not arise with objects, intensify with them, or disappear when they end. Awareness simply is—the constant background within which all auditory phenomena appear and vanish.

PRACTICE

- Sit in a location where various sounds occur naturally
- Close eyes to minimize visual distraction and enhance auditory sensitivity
- Rest in open receptivity to whatever auditory phenomena arise
- When a sound arises, follow its complete journey: notice arising, presence, and dissolution
- Throughout the sound arc, maintain awareness of the awareness witnessing the sound
- Recognize: Awareness remains even when sound has completely faded into silence
- When awareness becomes absorbed in thoughts, practice gentle return:
  - • No judgment of the wandering
  - • No forceful attempt to maintain sound awareness
  - • Simply allow awareness to disengage from thoughts and return to sounds
- If no sound is present when you return, rest in silence—recognizing that awareness of silence is still awareness
- As practice continues, begin recognizing not just sounds but the awareness that knows sounds

Proficiency Indicators
You're ready to progress when:

☐ You can follow complete sound arcs without becoming lost in thoughts about sounds

☐ Recognition emerges that awareness exists independent of sounds

☐ Returns to sound awareness become more effortless, requiring less deliberate effort

☐ Spontaneous moments arise where you recognize yourself as awareness observing sounds rather than identifying as a person hearing sounds

Key Understanding
Sound practice reveals the witnessing awareness more clearly than breath practice because sounds obviously exist as objects separate from you. This helps dissolve confusion between awareness (what you are) and experiences appearing within awareness (what you observe). Each gentle return strengthens this crucial distinction.

Practice Log
Session 1

Date: _____ Duration: _____

Key insights:

_____

_____

Session 2

Date: _____ Duration: _____

Key insights:

_____

_____

Session 3

Date: _____ Duration: _____

Key insights:

_____

_____

Session 4

Date: _____ Duration: _____

Key insights:

_____

_____

Session 5

Date: _____ Duration: _____

Key insights:

_____

_____

Session 6

Date: _____ Duration: _____

Key insights:

_____

_____

Visual Summary: The Three Levels of Mind

Draw or create a visual representation of how the wisdom you learned in this module relates in your own experience. Use any or all of the following: colors, symbols, hieroglyphs, codes, shapes, etc. in the open space below.

MODULE 18: The Complete Model of Mind and Consciousness - SYNTHESIS

Difficulty Level: ● Advanced

Commentary on Amenemopet Chapter 18

Daily Reflection Practice

Choose a verse from the Amenemopet Chapter 18 to work with each day.

Read Dr. Ashby's translation and commentary carefully. Then write your reflections about what this teaching means in your life today. How does it expose aryu patterns? What resistance arises? Where do you see this teaching reflected in your daily experiences?

Reflection 1

Date: _____ Verse: _____

My reflections:

_____

_____

_____

Reflection 2

Date: _____ Verse: _____

My reflections:

_____

_____

_____

Reflection 3

Date: _____   Verse: _____

My reflections:

_____

_____

_____

Reflection 4

Date: _____   Verse: _____

My reflections:

_____

_____

_____

Daily Contemplation Practice (15-20 minutes)

After your written reflection, sit in contemplation with a focus phrase from this module's teachings. Having practiced reflection, now sit while holding the meaning of the focus phrase. Holding is not continuing to reflect or think about it. Rather it means staying with the take-away meaning of the teaching for an extended period. You have already reflected; now stay with the meaning as you understand it currently. If the mind wanders, simply bring it back to the take-away objective of the focus phrase.

Focus Phrases for Contemplation

Choose one phrase to hold in contemplation:

- "Hat, ab, and Ab-Neter form complete consciousness model"
- "Kara (divine sanctuary) within contains Ab-Neter awaiting recognition"
- "All aspects of consciousness operate within Neberdjer"

Contemplation Practice Log

Session 1

Date: _____ Focus phrase used: _____

Insights:

_____

_____

Session 2

Date: _____ Focus phrase used: _____

Insights:

_____

_____

Session 3

Date: _____ Focus phrase used: _____

Insights:

_____

_____

Session 4

Date: _____ Focus phrase used: _____

Insights:

_____

_____

Session 5

Date: _____ Focus phrase used: _____

Insights:

_____

_____

Daily Meditation Practice (30-45 minutes)

LESSON 3: Visual Object (Apple) with Gentle Return

INSIGHT
Visual perception provides perhaps the clearest demonstration that you exist as awareness distinct from observed objects. When you place an apple before you and observe it, the relationship reveals undeniable truth: the apple exists as an object 'out there,' while you exist as the awareness 'in here' that knows the apple. This seemingly simple observation contains profound wisdom pointing toward your true nature.

PRACTICE
- Place a simple object (apple or other fruit) before you at comfortable viewing distance
- Sit comfortably with eyes open, gaze resting naturally on the object
- Observe the object's visual qualities without analysis: color, shape, texture
- Recognize: 'There is awareness of this apple'—the apple appears within awareness
- Notice: Are you the apple? Obviously not. You are the awareness observing the apple
- Recognize: Even if the apple disappears, awareness remains constant
- When thoughts about the apple arise ('This reminds me of...'), notice they are also objects in awareness
- Gently return from thought absorption to simple visual awareness of the object
- Gradually shift emphasis: less focus on the apple itself, more on the awareness observing
- After 10-15 minutes, remove the apple but maintain recognition that awareness continues
- Recognize: 'The awareness that observed the apple still exists—this is what I am'

Proficiency Indicators
You're ready to progress when:

☐ You can maintain visual awareness of object for 30-60 seconds, eventually several minutes

☐ Recognition emerges not just of the object but of the awareness observing the object

☐ The distinction between subject (you as awareness) and object (apple) becomes experientially clear

☐ When thoughts arise, you notice them more quickly and return to visual awareness with increasing gentleness

Key Understanding
This practice establishes the foundational recognition: you are the awareness in which experiences appear, not identical to any particular experience. The apple serves as training object helping consciousness recognize itself. Once this recognition stabilizes, any visual phenomenon can serve the same function.

Practice Log
Session 1

Date: Duration:

Key insights:

_____

_____

Session 2

Date: _____ Duration: _____

Key insights:

_____

_____

Session 3

Date: _____ Duration: _____

Key insights:

_____

_____

Session 4

Date: _____ Duration: _____

Key insights:

_____

_____

Session 5

Date: _____ Duration: _____

Key insights:

_____

_____

Session 6

Date: _____ Duration: _____

Key insights:

_____

_____

Visual Summary: The Three Levels of Mind

Draw or create a visual representation of how the wisdom you learned in this module relates in your own experience. Use any or all of the following: colors, symbols, hieroglyphs, codes, shapes, etc. in the open space below.

MODULE 19: The Glorification of Love Versus the Illusion of Power

Difficulty Level: Advanced

Commentary on Amenemopet Chapter 13

Daily Reflection Practice

Choose a verse from the Amenemopet Chapter 13 to work with each day.

Read Dr. Ashby's translation and commentary carefully. Then write your reflections about what this teaching means in your life today. How does it expose aryu patterns? What resistance arises? Where do you see this teaching reflected in your daily experiences?

Reflection 1

Date: _____ Verse: _____

My reflections:

_____

_____

_____

Reflection 2

Date: _____ Verse: _____

My reflections:

_____

_____

_____

Reflection 3

Date: _____ Verse: _____

My reflections:

_____

_____

_____

Reflection 4

Date: _____ Verse: _____

My reflections:

_____

_____

_____

Daily Contemplation Practice (15-20 minutes)

After your written reflection, sit in contemplation with a focus phrase from this module's teachings. Having practiced reflection, now sit while holding the meaning of the focus phrase. Holding is not continuing to reflect or think about it. Rather it means staying with the take-away meaning of the teaching for an extended period. You have already reflected; now stay with the meaning as you understand it currently. If the mind wanders, simply bring it back to the take-away objective of the focus phrase.

Focus Phrases for Contemplation

Choose one phrase to hold in contemplation:

- "Love aligned with divine consciousness glorifies existence"
- "True strength emerges from Ab-Neter connection"
- "Love operates as force thinning aryu density naturally"

Contemplation Practice Log

Session 1

Date: _____ Focus phrase used: _____

Insights:

_____

_____

Session 2

Date: _____ Focus phrase used: _____

Insights:

_____

_____

Session 3

Date: _____ Focus phrase used: _____

Insights:

_____

_____

Session 4

Date: _____ Focus phrase used: _____

Insights:

_____

_____

Session 5

Date: _____ Focus phrase used: _____

Insights:

_____

_____

Daily Meditation Practice (30-45 minutes)

LESSON 4: Body Sensation with Gentle Return

INSIGHT
Body sensations provide a particularly intimate gateway for developing gentle return practice because physical sensations arise continuously—subtle pressures, temperatures, tingles, tensions, the weight of limbs, contact of body with seat. Unlike breath (which follows cyclical pattern), sounds (which arise and dissolve), or visual objects (which remain stable), body sensations present a constantly shifting field of phenomena, offering continuous opportunities for practicing recognition and return.

PRACTICE
- Sit comfortably with eyes closed
- Begin with feet: notice any sensations—tingling, warmth, pressure, pulsing
- Move attention slowly up through body: ankles, calves, knees, thighs
- Continue through abdomen, chest, shoulders, arms, hands, neck, face, head
- Don't create sensations—simply notice what's already present
- After completing systematic scan, expand to whole-body awareness simultaneously
- Recognize: Something is aware of these sensations—what is this awareness?
- Notice: Awareness observing sensations has no physical qualities yet clearly exists
- When absorbed in thoughts, practice gentle return to somatic awareness
- When discomfort arises, observe both sensation and mental reaction to it
- Gradually emphasize less the specific sensations, more the awareness knowing them

Proficiency Indicators
You're ready to progress when:

☐ You can complete full body scan maintaining awareness without constant thought intrusion

☐ Recognition emerges that sensations come and go while awareness remains constant

☐ Impulse to react immediately to every discomfort decreases

☐ Spontaneous whole-body awareness arises during daily activities—washing dishes, walking, working

Key Understanding
Body sensation practice serves dual purposes: it grounds awareness in present-moment reality (opposing habitual tendency toward abstract thought absorption), and it reveals that you exist as awareness observing the body rather than being identical to physical form.

Practice Log
Session 1

Date: _____ Duration: _____

Key insights:

_____

_____

Session 2

Date: _____ Duration: _____

Key insights:

_____

_____

Session 3

Date: _____ Duration: _____

Key insights:

_____

_____

Session 4

Date: _____ Duration: _____

Key insights:

_____

_____

Session 5

Date: _____ Duration: _____

Key insights:

_____

_____

Session 6

Date: _____ Duration: _____

Key insights:

_____

_____

Visual Summary: The Three Levels of Mind

Draw or create a visual representation of how the wisdom you learned in this module relates in your own experience. Use any or all of the following: colors, symbols, hieroglyphs, codes, shapes, etc. in the open space below.

MODULE 20: The All-Seeing Eye of Cosmic Mind

Difficulty Level: ● Advanced

Commentary on Amenemopet Chapter 15

Daily Reflection Practice

Choose a verse from the Amenemopet Chapter 15 to work with each day.

Read Dr. Ashby's translation and commentary carefully. Then write your reflections about what this teaching means in your life today. How does it expose aryu patterns? What resistance arises? Where do you see this teaching reflected in your daily experiences?

Reflection 1

Date: _____ Verse: _____

My reflections:

_____

_____

_____

Reflection 2

Date: _____ Verse: _____

My reflections:

_____

_____

_____

Reflection 3

Date: _____ Verse: _____

My reflections:

_____

_____

_____

Reflection 4

Date: _____ Verse: _____

My reflections:

_____

_____

_____

Daily Contemplation Practice (15-20 minutes)

After your written reflection, sit in contemplation with a focus phrase from this module's teachings. Having practiced reflection, now sit while holding the meaning of the focus phrase. Holding is not continuing to reflect or think about it. Rather it means staying with the take-away meaning of the teaching for an extended period. You have already reflected; now stay with the meaning as you understand it currently. If the mind wanders, simply bring it back to the take-away objective of the focus phrase.

Focus Phrases for Contemplation

Choose one phrase to hold in contemplation:

- "Divine consciousness (Neberdjer) sees all actions, thoughts, feelings"
- "Living with awareness of divine observation purifies intentions"
- "Recognition of divine witness supports ethical transformation"

Contemplation Practice Log

Session 1

Date: _____ Focus phrase used: _____

Insights:

_____

_____

Session 2

Date: _____ Focus phrase used: _____

Insights:

_____

_____

Session 3

Date: _____ Focus phrase used: _____

Insights:

_____

_____

Session 4

Date: _____ Focus phrase used: _____

Insights:

_____

_____

Session 5

Date: _____ Focus phrase used: _____

Insights:

_____

_____

Daily Meditation Practice (30-45 minutes)

LESSON 5: Thought Observation with Gentle Return

INSIGHT

Thought observation represents the most challenging yet most significant modality because thoughts constitute the very substance of identification that creates the sense of separate self. Until consciousness learns to observe thoughts as objects appearing within awareness (rather than identifying with thoughts as self), all other observation practices remain incomplete.

PRACTICE

- Sit with eyes closed, no specific focal object
- Simply observe: What thoughts arise right now?
- When a thought appears, recognize: 'A thought is present'
- Notice: The thought is an object; awareness witnessing it is the subject
- Don't engage with thought content—don't follow, analyze, or elaborate
- Simply note 'thinking' and allow the thought to dissolve naturally
- When absorbed in extended thought chains, practice gentle return
- Notice gaps between thoughts—brief moments of mental silence
- Rest in the gap without trying to prolong it forcefully
- Recognize: Throughout all thinking and non-thinking, awareness never stopped existing

Proficiency Indicators

You're ready to progress when:

☐ You notice thought identification more quickly—within seconds rather than minutes

☐ The distinction between thoughts (objects) and awareness (witness) becomes experientially clear

☐ Gaps between thoughts become more noticeable

☐ Meta-awareness develops: capacity to be aware that you are aware of thinking

☐ You recognize the same observing awareness operates in all modalities (breath, sound, body, thoughts)

Key Understanding

Thought observation trains awareness to observe the very phenomena that typically create identification. The practice reveals that you are not identical to thoughts; you are the awareness within which thoughts appear and dissolve.

Practice Log

Session 1

Date: _____ Duration: _____

Key insights:

_____

_____

Session 2

Date: _____ Duration: _____

Key insights:

_____

_____

Session 3

Date: _____ Duration: _____

Key insights:

_____

_____

Session 4

Date: _____ Duration: _____

Key insights:

_____

_____

Session 5

Date: _____ Duration: _____

Key insights:

_____

_____

Session 6

Date: _____ Duration: _____

Key insights:

_____

_____

Visual Summary: The Three Levels of Mind

Draw or create a visual representation of how the wisdom you learned in this module relates in your own experience. Use any or all of the following: colors, symbols, hieroglyphs, codes, shapes, etc. in the open space below.

MODULE 21: The Psychology of Luxury Attachment

Difficulty Level: ● Advanced

Commentary on Amenemopet Chapter 16

Daily Reflection Practice

Choose a verse from the Amenemopet Chapter 16 to work with each day.

Read Dr. Ashby's translation and commentary carefully. Then write your reflections about what this teaching means in your life today. How does it expose aryu patterns? What resistance arises? Where do you see this teaching reflected in your daily experiences?

Reflection 1

Date: _____ Verse: _____

My reflections:

_____

_____

_____

Reflection 2

Date: _____ Verse: _____

My reflections:

_____

_____

_____

Reflection 3

Date: _____ Verse: _____

My reflections:

_____

_____

_____

Reflection 4

Date: _____ Verse: _____

My reflections:

_____

_____

_____

Daily Contemplation Practice (15-20 minutes)

After your written reflection, sit in contemplation with a focus phrase from this module's teachings. Having practiced reflection, now sit while holding the meaning of the focus phrase. Holding is not continuing to reflect or think about it. Rather it means staying with the take-away meaning of the teaching for an extended period. You have already reflected; now stay with the meaning as you understand it currently. If the mind wanders, simply bring it back to the take-away objective of the focus phrase.

Focus Phrases for Contemplation

Choose one phrase to hold in contemplation:

- "Freedom from luxury-attachment reveals inherent fulfillment within"
- "Simplicity supports clarity"
- "True wealth resides in Ab-Neter awareness"

Contemplation Practice Log

Session 1

Date: _____ Focus phrase used: _____

Insights:

_____

_____

Session 2

Date: _____ Focus phrase used: _____

Insights:

_____

_____

Session 3

Date: _____ Focus phrase used: _____

Insights:

_____

_____

Session 4

Date: _____ Focus phrase used: _____

Insights:

_____

_____

Session 5

Date: _____ Focus phrase used: _____

Insights:

_____

_____

Daily Meditation Practice (30-45 minutes)

LESSON 6: Recognition of the Witness Itself

INSIGHT

Having practiced gentle return with five modalities (breath, sound, visual objects, body, thoughts), the practice now undergoes fundamental transformation: instead of emphasizing objects being observed, consciousness turns toward recognizing the observer itself. This shift represents the transition from concentration practices (Stages I-II) toward recognition practices (Stages III+).

PRACTICE

- Begin with 5 minutes of any previous practice to settle mind
- Shift attention from observed objects toward the observer itself
- Ask: 'What is aware right now?' (Not thinking about awareness—recognizing it directly)
- Notice: This awareness has no form, color, location—yet it clearly exists
- Maintain recognition: 'I am this awareness, not the phenomena appearing within it'
- When thoughts arise, ask: 'What is aware of this thought?'
- When sensations occur, ask: 'What is aware of this sensation?'
- Each question returns consciousness to recognition of witnessing awareness
- As practice deepens, questioning may become unnecessary—direct recognition emerges
- Maintain continuous recognition of awareness for extended periods (10-20 minutes)
- Notice the non-dual hint: observer and observed exist within same consciousness

Proficiency Indicators

You're ready to progress when:

☐ You can recognize witnessing awareness directly rather than merely knowing about it conceptually

☐ Periods emerge where you rest as awareness for 30-60 seconds before absorption occurs

☐ When objects arise, you can maintain recognition: 'I am the awareness knowing this'

☐ Return to witness recognition becomes more effortless

☐ You begin noticing witness awareness spontaneously during daily activities

Key Understanding

This practice establishes the foundation for all subsequent Sau Neberdjer development. Recognition of witnessing awareness—the Soul-Aware-Witness-Self—represents the pivotal shift from being lost in phenomena to recognizing what you essentially are.

Practice Log

Session 1

Date: _____ Duration: _____

Key insights:

_____

_____

Session 2

Date: _____ Duration: _____

Key insights:

_____

_____

Session 3

Date: _____ Duration: _____

Key insights:

_____

_____

Session 4

Date: _____ Duration: _____

Key insights:

_____

_____

Session 5

Date: _____ Duration: _____

Key insights:

_____

_____

Session 6

Date: _____ Duration: _____

Key insights:

_____

_____

Visual Summary: The Three Levels of Mind

Draw or create a visual representation of how the wisdom you learned in this module relates in your own experience. Use any or all of the following: colors, symbols, hieroglyphs, codes, shapes, etc. in the open space below.

MODULE 22: The Psychology of Volitional Fraud

Difficulty Level: ● Advanced

Commentary on Amenemopet Chapter 17

Daily Reflection Practice

Choose a verse from the Amenemopet Chapter 17 to work with each day.

Read Dr. Ashby's translation and commentary carefully. Then write your reflections about what this teaching means in your life today. How does it expose aryu patterns? What resistance arises? Where do you see this teaching reflected in your daily experiences?

Reflection 1

Date: _____ Verse: _____

My reflections:

_____

_____

_____

Reflection 2

Date: _____ Verse: _____

My reflections:

_____

_____

_____

Reflection 3

Date: _____ Verse: _____

My reflections:

_____

_____

_____

Reflection 4

Date: _____ Verse: _____

My reflections:

_____

_____

_____

Daily Contemplation Practice (15-20 minutes)

After your written reflection, sit in contemplation with a focus phrase from this module's teachings. Having practiced reflection, now sit while holding the meaning of the focus phrase. Holding is not continuing to reflect or think about it. Rather it means staying with the take-away meaning of the teaching for an extended period. You have already reflected; now stay with the meaning as you understand it currently. If the mind wanders, simply bring it back to the take-away objective of the focus phrase.

Focus Phrases for Contemplation

Choose one phrase to hold in contemplation:

- "Fraud perpetrated through deliberate volition creates severe aryu consequences"
- "Truth-in-action aligns consciousness with cosmic order (Maat)"
- "Integrity maintained through all circumstances supports purification"

Contemplation Practice Log

Session 1

Date: _____ Focus phrase used: _____

Insights:

_____

_____

Session 2

Date: _____ Focus phrase used: _____

Insights:

_____

_____

Session 3

Date: _____ Focus phrase used: _____

Insights:

_____

_____

Session 4

Date: _____ Focus phrase used: _____

Insights:

_____

_____

Session 5

Date: _____ Focus phrase used: _____

Insights:

_____

_____

Daily Meditation Practice (30-45 minutes)

LESSON 7: Gap Extension Between Thoughts

INSIGHT

Having established capacity for recognizing witnessing awareness (Lesson 6), the practice now works specifically with gaps between thoughts—those brief moments of mental silence when one thought has ended and the next has not yet begun. These gaps reveal consciousness in its natural state, temporarily free from identification with mental content.

PRACTICE

- Sit with eyes closed, no specific focal object
- Begin with thought observation (Lesson 5): simply notice thoughts arising
- Direct attention specifically to transitions between thoughts
- When one thought ends, notice the gap before the next thought begins
- Don't attempt to create or prolong gaps forcefully
- Simply remain present in gaps when they naturally occur
- Recognize: In the gap, awareness exists without thoughts
- Notice the quality of awareness in gaps—luminous presence, not empty blankness
- Practice non-engagement with thought content to allow gaps to emerge more frequently
- When absorbed in extended thought chains, practice gentle return
- Begin recognizing gaps in daily life: completing one task... brief gap... beginning next

Proficiency Indicators
You're ready to progress when:

☐ You recognize gaps between thoughts regularly during formal practice

☐ Gap duration naturally extends without force—from 1-2 seconds to 5-10 seconds

☐ Quality of gaps shifts from empty blankness to luminous presence

☐ Spontaneous gap recognition begins occurring during daily activities

☐ Thought chains shorten significantly

☐ You recognize awareness present in gaps as identical to awareness present when thoughts occur

Key Understanding
Gap extension practice reveals that consciousness exists independent of mental content—awareness remains whether thoughts are present or absent. This recognition provides experiential foundation for understanding Ab Neter (divine consciousness) as your true nature beyond all mental modifications.

Practice Log
Session 1

Date: _____ Duration: _____

Key insights:

_____

_____

Session 2

Date: _____ Duration: _____

Key insights:

_____

_____

Session 3

Date: _____ Duration: _____

Key insights:

_____

_____

Session 4

Date: _____ Duration: _____

Key insights:

_____

_____

Session 5

Date: _____ Duration: _____

Key insights:

_____

_____

Session 6

Date: _____ Duration: _____

Key insights:

_____

_____

Visual Summary: The Three Levels of Mind

Draw or create a visual representation of how the wisdom you learned in this module relates in your own experience. Use any or all of the following: colors, symbols, hieroglyphs, codes, shapes, etc. in the open space below.

MODULE 23: The Illusion of Self-Will and Divine Guidance

Difficulty Level: Advanced

Commentary on Amenemopet Chapter 18

Daily Reflection Practice

Choose a verse from the Amenemopet Chapter 18 to work with each day.

Read Dr. Ashby's translation and commentary carefully. Then write your reflections about what this teaching means in your life today. How does it expose aryu patterns? What resistance arises? Where do you see this teaching reflected in your daily experiences?

Reflection 1

Date: _____ Verse: _____

My reflections:

_____

_____

_____

Reflection 2

Date: _____ Verse: _____

My reflections:

_____

_____

_____

Reflection 3

Date: _____ Verse: _____

My reflections:

_____

_____

_____

Reflection 4

Date: _____ Verse: _____

My reflections:

_____

_____

_____

Daily Contemplation Practice (15-20 minutes)

After your written reflection, sit in contemplation with a focus phrase from this module's teachings. Having practiced reflection, now sit while holding the meaning of the focus phrase. Holding is not continuing to reflect or think about it. Rather it means staying with the take-away meaning of the teaching for an extended period. You have already reflected; now stay with the meaning as you understand it currently. If the mind wanders, simply bring it back to the take-away objective of the focus phrase.

Focus Phrases for Contemplation

Choose one phrase to hold in contemplation:

- "Divine guidance operates through Ab-Neter"
- "Trust in providence aligns with cosmic flow"
- "Illusion of separation is dissolved through trusting divine providence"

Contemplation Practice Log

Session 1

Date: _____ Focus phrase used: _____

Insights:

_____

_____

Session 2

Date: _____ Focus phrase used: _____

Insights:

_____

_____

Session 3

Date: _____ Focus phrase used: _____

Insights:

_____

_____

Session 4

Date: _____ Focus phrase used: _____

Insights:

_____

_____

Session 5

Date: _____ Focus phrase used: _____

Insights:

_____

_____

Daily Meditation Practice (30-45 minutes)

LESSON 8: Awareness Independent of Objects

INSIGHT

This lesson develops capacity for resting as awareness without dependence on any phenomenal anchor—no breath, no sounds, no visual objects, no body scan, no thought observation. The practice cultivates what might be called 'objectless awareness' or 'awareness aware of itself'—consciousness recognizing its own existence independent of all content.

PRACTICE

- Sit with eyes closed
- Begin with 5-10 minutes of witness recognition (Lesson 6) to establish awareness
- Gradually release attention from all specific objects
- Rest as awareness itself—not awareness of something, just awareness
- When perceptions arise (sounds, sensations, thoughts), recognize: 'I am aware of this'
- Emphasis rests not on the object but on the 'I am aware'
- Maintain continuous recognition of awareness for extended periods
- When absorbed in objects, ask: 'What is aware right now?'
- Notice: Observer and observed exist within same consciousness
- Allow the distinction between awareness and phenomena to soften naturally

Proficiency Indicators

You're ready to progress when:

☐ You can recognize witnessing awareness directly

☐ Periods emerge where you rest as awareness for 30-60 seconds

☐ When objects arise, you maintain recognition: 'I am the awareness knowing this'

☐ Return to witness recognition becomes effortless

☐ You notice witness awareness spontaneously during daily activities

☐ The non-dual hint emerges: all appears within one consciousness

Key Understanding

This practice represents the culmination of the recognition pathway, where consciousness recognizes itself as the constant background of all experience—neither created by phenomena nor dependent on them for its existence.

Practice Log

Session 1

Date: _____ Duration: _____

Key insights:

_____

_____

Session 2

Date: _____ Duration: _____

Key insights:

_____

_____

Session 3

Date: _____ Duration: _____

Key insights:

_____

_____

Session 4

Date: _____ Duration: _____

Key insights:

_____

_____

Session 5

Date: _____ Duration: _____

Key insights:

_____

_____

Session 6

Date: _____ Duration: _____

Key insights:

_____

_____

Visual Summary: The Three Levels of Mind

Draw or create a visual representation of how the wisdom you learned in this module relates in your own experience. Use any or all of the following: colors, symbols, hieroglyphs, codes, shapes, etc. in the open space below.

MODULE 24: Balance Between Trust and Righteous Action

Difficulty Level: ● Advanced

Commentary on Amenemopet Chapter 21

Daily Reflection Practice

Choose a verse from the Amenemopet Chapter 21 to work with each day.

Read Dr. Ashby's translation and commentary carefully. Then write your reflections about what this teaching means in your life today. How does it expose aryu patterns? What resistance arises? Where do you see this teaching reflected in your daily experiences?

Reflection 1

Date: _____ Verse: _____

My reflections:

_____

_____

_____

Reflection 2

Date: _____ Verse: _____

My reflections:

_____

_____

_____

Reflection 3

Date: _____ Verse: _____

My reflections:

_____

_____

_____

Reflection 4

Date: _____ Verse: _____

My reflections:

_____

_____

_____

Daily Contemplation Practice (15-20 minutes)

After your written reflection, sit in contemplation with a focus phrase from this module's teachings. Having practiced reflection, now sit while holding the meaning of the focus phrase. Holding is not continuing to reflect or think about it. Rather it means staying with the take-away meaning of the teaching for an extended period. You have already reflected; now stay with the meaning as you understand it currently. If the mind wanders, simply bring it back to the take-away objective of the focus phrase.

Focus Phrases for Contemplation

Choose one phrase to hold in contemplation:

- "Trust in divine providence balanced with personal righteous effort"
- "Action without divine alignment wastes vital energy"
- "Righteous action performed while trusting outcome to providence"

Contemplation Practice Log

Session 1

Date: _____ Focus phrase used: _____

Insights:

_____

_____

Session 2

Date: _____ Focus phrase used: _____

Insights:

_____

_____

Session 3

Date: _____ Focus phrase used: _____

Insights:

_____

_____

Session 4

Date: _____ Focus phrase used: _____

Insights:

_____

_____

Session 5

Date: _____ Focus phrase used: _____

Insights:

_____

_____

Daily Meditation Practice (30-45 minutes)

LESSON 9: Prolonged Ab-Neter Recognition

INSIGHT

Having established capacity for witness consciousness recognition, the practice now focuses on recognizing Ab Neter—the divine consciousness that sustains your capacity to be aware. This represents transition from recognizing awareness as 'mine' (individual witness) to recognizing awareness as divine (universal consciousness manifesting individually).

PRACTICE

- Begin with witness recognition practice (Lesson 6-8) for 10-15 minutes
- Establish stable recognition: 'I am awareness, not phenomena'
- Now deepen recognition: contemplate 'What sustains this awareness?'
- Recognize: Awareness exists not through your effort but as divine gift
- This is Ab Neter—divine consciousness within, your portion of Neberdjer
- Rest in Ab Neter recognition: awareness recognizing its divine nature
- When thoughts arise: 'Ab Neter is aware of this thought'
- When sensations occur: 'Ab Neter experiences this through body-mind'
- Maintain prolonged Ab-Neter recognition (20-30 minutes)
- Practice gentle returns from egoic identification back to Ab-Neter recognition

Proficiency Indicators
You're ready to progress when:

☐ You can maintain Ab-Neter recognition for 15-30+ minutes

☐ Practice shifts from 'I am trying to recognize' to 'Resting as Ab-Neter'

☐ Personal ownership over awareness decreases

☐ Spontaneous Ab-Neter recognition occurs during daily life

☐ Fear of death decreases—recognition deepens that Ab-Neter exists beyond body

☐ Values shift: urgent concerns lose compelling quality as consciousness recognizes itself as divine

Key Understanding
Ab-Neter recognition represents the ultimate Prologue goal: discovering the divine sanctuary (kara) within. This practice does not create Ab-Neter—divine consciousness has always sustained awareness. Rather, practice removes aryu-based identifications that obscured recognition of your true nature.

Practice Log
Session 1

Date: _____ Duration: _____

Key insights:

_____

_____

Session 2

Date: _____ Duration: _____

Key insights:

_____

_____

Session 3

Date: _____ Duration: _____

Key insights:

_____

_____

Session 4

Date: _____ Duration: _____

Key insights:

_____

_____

Session 5

Date: _____ Duration: _____

Key insights:

_____

_____

Session 6

Date: _____ Duration: _____

Key insights:

_____

_____

Visual Summary: The Three Levels of Mind

Draw or create a visual representation of how the wisdom you learned in this module relates in your own experience. Use any or all of the following: colors, symbols, hieroglyphs, codes, shapes, etc. in the open space below.

MODULE 25: Compassionate Treatment of the Vulnerable

Difficulty Level: ● Advanced - DAILY LIFE INTEGRATION

Commentary on Amenemopet Chapter 25

Daily Reflection Practice

Choose a verse from the Amenemopet Chapter 25 to work with each day.

Read Dr. Ashby's translation and commentary carefully. Then write your reflections about what this teaching means in your life today. How does it expose aryu patterns? What resistance arises? Where do you see this teaching reflected in your daily experiences?

Reflection 1

Date: _____ Verse: _____

My reflections:

_____

_____

_____

Reflection 2

Date: _____ Verse: _____

My reflections:

_____

_____

_____

Reflection 3

Date: _____ Verse: _____

My reflections:

_____

_____

_____

Reflection 4

Date: _____ Verse: _____

My reflections:

_____

_____

_____

Daily Contemplation Practice (15-20 minutes)

After your written reflection, sit in contemplation with a focus phrase from this module's teachings. Having practiced reflection, now sit while holding the meaning of the focus phrase. Holding is not continuing to reflect or think about it. Rather it means staying with the take-away meaning of the teaching for an extended period. You have already reflected; now stay with the meaning as you understand it currently. If the mind wanders, simply bring it back to the take-away objective of the focus phrase.

Focus Phrases for Contemplation

Choose one phrase to hold in contemplation:

- "Compassion toward vulnerable beings reflects Ab-Neter awareness"
- "Protection of vulnerable generates positive aryu supporting spiritual growth"
- "Divine consciousness recognizes itself in all beings"

Contemplation Practice Log

Session 1

Date: _____ Focus phrase used: _____

Insights:

_____

_____

Session 2

Date: _____ Focus phrase used: _____

Insights:

_____

_____

Session 3

Date: _____ Focus phrase used: _____

Insights:

_____

_____

Session 4

Date: _____ Focus phrase used: _____

Insights:

_____

_____

Session 5

Date: _____ Focus phrase used: _____

Insights:

_____

_____

Daily Meditation Practice (45-60 minutes)

LESSON 10 PARTS A-C: Daily Life Integration

Lesson 10 extends Sau-Neberdjer recognition beyond formal meditation into continuous practice throughout all daily activities. This represents the mature fruition of gentle return practice—consciousness maintaining recognition whether sitting formally, working, relating to others, or engaging in any activity.

PART A: Transition Moments

Practice gentle return during natural transitions:

- Waking up: Before engaging thoughts, recognize awareness present
- Finishing one activity... brief gap... beginning next: Notice awareness in transition
- Entering/exiting spaces: Doorways as awareness triggers
- Before meals: Pause to recognize awareness before eating
- Completing tasks: Brief recognition before moving to next activity

PART B: During Routine Activities

Maintain awareness during daily tasks:

- Walking: Recognize awareness of body moving through space
- Eating: Notice awareness experiencing tastes, textures, sensations
- Washing: Recognize awareness knowing water, soap, physical sensations
- Working: Periodic recognition—'Ab-Neter is aware through this activity'
- Driving: Awareness recognizing itself while engaging complex task

PART C: In Relationships

Practice awareness recognition during interactions:

- Before speaking: Brief recognition—'Ab-Neter is about to speak through this form'
- While listening: Recognize awareness hearing words without becoming absorbed in reactions
- During conflicts: Maintain witness awareness observing emotions arising
- In intimacy: Recognition that two bodies, one awareness
- With strangers: Brief recognition that same consciousness manifests in all forms

Practice Log for Module 25

Week 1

Transition moments where I practiced recognition: _____

Activities where awareness maintained: _____

Relationship moments where witness consciousness operated: _____

Key insights:

_____

_____

Week 2

Transition moments where I practiced recognition: _____

Activities where awareness maintained: _____

Relationship moments where witness consciousness operated: _____

Key insights:

_____

_____

Week 3

Transition moments where I practiced recognition: _____

Activities where awareness maintained: _____

Relationship moments where witness consciousness operated: _____

Key insights:

_____

_____

Week 4

Transition moments where I practiced recognition: _____

Activities where awareness maintained: _____

Relationship moments where witness consciousness operated: _____

Key insights:

_____

_____

Week 5

Transition moments where I practiced recognition: _____

Activities where awareness maintained: _____

Relationship moments where witness consciousness operated: _____

Key insights:

_____

_____

Week 6

Transition moments where I practiced recognition: _____

Activities where awareness maintained: _____

Relationship moments where witness consciousness operated: _____

Key insights:

_____

_____

Visual Summary: The Three Levels of Mind

Draw or create a visual representation of how the wisdom you learned in this module relates in your own experience. Use any or all of the following: colors, symbols, hieroglyphs, codes, shapes, etc. in the open space below.

MODULE 26: The Path from Humility to Vigilant Serenity

Difficulty Level: ● Advanced - COMPLETION MODULE

Commentary on Amenemopet Chapter 26

Daily Reflection Practice

Choose a verse from the Amenemopet Chapter 26 to work with each day.

Read Dr. Ashby's translation and commentary carefully. Then write your reflections about what this teaching means in your life today. How does it expose aryu patterns? What resistance arises? Where do you see this teaching reflected in your daily experiences?

Reflection 1

Date: _____ Verse: _____

My reflections:

_____

_____

_____

Reflection 2

Date: _____ Verse: _____

My reflections:

_____

_____

_____

Reflection 3

Date: _____ Verse: _____

My reflections:

_____

_____

_____

Reflection 4

Date: _____ Verse: _____

My reflections:

_____

_____

_____

Daily Contemplation Practice (15-20 minutes)

After your written reflection, sit in contemplation with a focus phrase from this module's teachings. Having practiced reflection, now sit while holding the meaning of the focus phrase. Holding is not continuing to reflect or think about it. Rather it means staying with the take-away meaning of the teaching for an extended period. You have already reflected; now stay with the meaning as you understand it currently. If the mind wanders, simply bring it back to the take-away objective of the focus phrase.

Focus Phrases for Contemplation

Choose one phrase to hold in contemplation:

- "Humility opens pathway to divine sanctuary (kara) within"
- "Vigilant serenity maintains Ab-Neter awareness amid life's turbulence"
- "Silent mind and feelings represent mature fruit of purification practice"

Contemplation Practice Log
Session 1

Date: _____ Focus phrase used: _____

Insights:

_____

_____

Session 2

Date: _____ Focus phrase used: _____

Insights:

_____

_____

Session 3

Date: _____ Focus phrase used: _____

Insights:

_____

_____

Session 4

Date: _____ Focus phrase used: _____

Insights:

_____

_____

Session 5

Date: _____ Focus phrase used: _____

Insights:

_____

_____

Daily Meditation Practice (45-60 minutes)

LESSON 10 PARTS D-E: Advanced Integration & Path Completion

PART D: Challenge-Based Recognition
Maintain awareness recognition especially during difficult moments:

- When anger arises: Recognize 'Awareness is observing anger arising in body-mind'
- When fear emerges: Notice 'Ab-Neter witnesses fear without being threatened by it'
- When craving pulls: Observe 'Desire is an object appearing within awareness'
- When judgment occurs: Recognize 'Critical thoughts arise within witnessing consciousness'
- When pain manifests: Notice 'Awareness knows pain without being pain itself'

PART E: Gratitude & Recognition Practice
Cultivate gratitude for consciousness itself:

- Morning: 'Gratitude for awareness returning with waking'
- Midday: 'Gratitude that awareness continues throughout all activities'
- Evening: 'Gratitude for consciousness that never actually sleeps'
- Before sleep: 'Gratitude for Ab-Neter sustaining capacity to be aware'
- Difficult moments: 'Gratitude that awareness witnesses suffering without being destroyed by it'

PATH COMPLETION REFLECTION

You have now completed all 26 modules and 10 Gentle Return lessons. Take time to recognize your journey:

What You've Accomplished:

✓ Developed capacity for sustained meditation (45-60 minutes)

✓ Established witness consciousness recognition

✓ Recognized Ab-Neter as your divine nature

✓ Extended practice from formal sessions into daily life

✓ Learned to return gently from identification countless times

✓ Begun the transformation from heated to silent mind and feelings

The Path Forward:

Completing this guidebook does not mean mastery—it means you now understand the complete framework and have practices that will deepen throughout life.

- Continue daily formal practice (45-60 minutes minimum)
- Maintain gentle return practice throughout all activities
- Return to challenging modules when aryu patterns re-emerge
- Study Dr. Ashby's complete book for deeper understanding
- Seek guidance from qualified teachers
- Recognize: The journey continues; each moment offers opportunity for recognition

May You Realize:

- The vital-life-fire (udja) that purifies consciousness
- The kara—divine sanctuary where Ab-Neter resides
- Your essential nature as consciousness itself
- Ab-Neter as Neberdjer expressing through your form
- The silent peace that passes understanding
- Earthly well-being through divine wisdom
- Liberation from aryu-dominated reactivity
- Recognition of consciousness as your true identity

Ankh Udja Seneb

(Life, Vitality, Health)

The Journey of Transformation Continues...

www.ingramcontent.com/pod-product-compliance
Lightning Source LLC
Chambersburg PA
CBHW081442070526
44586CB00019B/2207